Trade in Services Negotiations

Trade in Services Negotiations

A Guide for Developing Countries

Edited by Sebastián Sáez

THE WORLD BANK
Washington, D.C.

© 2010 The International Bank for Reconstruction and Development / The World Bank
1818 H Street NW
Washington DC 20433
Telephone: 202-473-1000
Internet: www.worldbank.org
E-mail: feedback@worldbank.org

ISBN: 978-0-8213-8410-7
eISBN: 978-0-8213-8411-4
DOI: 10.1596/978-0-8213-8410-7

Library of Congress Cataloging-in-Publication Data has been applied for

Cover photo © Comstock/Corbis.
Cover design by Quantum Think.

Contents

List of Contributors   *ix*
Foreword   *xi*
Acknowledgments   *xiii*
Abbreviations   *xv*

Chapter 1   **The Strategic Development Role of Trade in Services** 1
             Sebastián Sáez

             Why This Book?   4
             Understanding the Strategic Nature of
                 Liberalization   6
             The Strategic Role of International Agreements
                 in Services   11
             Notes   14
             References   15

Chapter 2   **Negotiating Trade in Services: A Practical Guide
             for Developing Countries**   19
             Mario Marconini and Pierre Sauvé

             Introduction   19

Mapping a Strategy for Services in National
    Development Plans   21
Preparing for Service Negotiations   25
Conducting Service Negotiations   44
Enhancing the Capacity to Supply   63
The Challenge of Aid for Trade in Services   76
Conclusion   81
Notes   81
References   84

Chapter 3   **The Negotiation and Management of Regulations
               in the Trade in Services**   87
               Sebastián Sáez and Marcel Vaillant

Understanding Service Regulations: The Basic
    Components of SERET   88
Building SERET: The Positive List Approach   101
The Case of PTAs and the Negative List Approach   109
Conclusions   112
Annex 3A Statistics on Service Agreements   113
Notes   115
References   116

Chapter 4   **Liberalization in the Trade in Services:
               A Negotiation Exercise**   121
               Sebastián Sáez and Anna Lanoszka

The Trade Dimension of Logistics Services   123
The Trade Dimension of Health Services   134
Trade in Services: A Negotiation Exercise   147
Annex 4A Health-Related Services   163
Notes   168
References   168

Index   171

Boxes

2.1   The Place of Services in National Development Strategies   24
2.2   The Policy-Making Benefits of Effective Intragovernmental
       Coordination   28

2.3   Performing a Trade-Related Regulatory Audit in Services   37
2.4   Illustrative Examples of Trade-Related Regulatory Audits   41
2.5   Key Questions during the Preparatory Phase of Service
       Negotiations   43
2.6   The Doha Round Shift toward Collective Requests   47
2.7   Concerns Arising in Service Negotiations   54
2.8   Examples of Best Practice Capacity Building in Services   59
2.9   Best Practices in Trade-Related Training: Course Design
       and Delivery   62
2.10   The Implementation Phase of the Service Trade
       Negotiation Cycle   64
2.11   The Strengths and Weaknesses of Domestic Suppliers   67
2.12   Organizing Service Coalitions in Developing Countries   69
2.13   Providing Market Intelligence to Developing-Country
       Suppliers: The Trade Facilitation Office, Canada   73
2.14   Strengthening the Supply-Side Capacity of
       Developing-Country Exporters   75
2.15   Addressing Aid for Trade in Services: The
       CARIFORUM–European Community Economic
       Partnership Agreement   78
3.1   Sector Classification   89
3.2   Annex 1: Type of Reservation: United States–Chile
       Free Trade Agreement   111

Figures
2.1   Checklist for Trade Policy Formulation, Thailand   34
2.2   Negotiating Essentials: Interagency Coordination and
       External Stakeholder Consultations   35
4.1   Overperformers and Underperformers: Gross National
       Income per Capita and the Logistics Performance Index   124

Tables
1.1   Analytical Structure for the Description of Service
       Regulations   9
2.1   Sample List of Exporters and Other Domestic
       Stakeholders in Selected Service Sectors   31
2.2   Factors to Consider in Formulating a Request or Offer   50
3.1   Reasons, Objectives, and Instruments of Regulation in
       Selected Service Sectors   90
3.2   Discrimination and Rules   90

3.3	Foreign Suppliers and Types of Impact: Discriminatory and Nondiscriminatory Restrictions	91
3.4	Modes of Supply and the GATS	92
3.5	Schedule of GATS Commitments	93
3.6	Comparative Coverage of Rules in GATT and the GATS, Market Access Modes	94
3.7	PTAs to Achieve Service Liberalization	100
3.8	An Example of a Service Schedule	102
3.9	First Commitment Schedule Downloaded	104
3.10	Pasting the W/120 Code for Each Mode of Supply in the Subsector	106
3.11	Nesting Horizontal Commitments	107
3A.1	Service Trade Agreements by Type, Hub Country, Partner, and WTO Notification Year	113
4.1	Trade in Logistics Services: Examples of Restrictions	127
4.2	Freight Logistics Checklist	132
4.3	Logistics Services: Issues in the Development of Negotiating Positions	135
4.4	The Modes of Trade in the Health Sector	139
4.5	Health Service Trade: Issues to Consider in Developing Negotiating Positions	144
4A.1.	Health-Related Services: Relevant Sectors and the Corresponding CPC Classifications	163

List of Contributors

About the Editor

Sebastián Saéz, Senior Trade Economist, International Trade Department, Poverty Reduction and Economic Management, World Bank.

About the Contributors

Anna Lanoszka, Professor of International Economic Relations, University of Windsor, Ontario, Canada.

Mario Marconini from Manatt Jones Marconini, São Paulo, Brazil.

Pierre Sauvé, World Trade Institute, Berne, Switzerland.

Marcel Vaillant, Professor International Trade, Economic Department, Universidad de la República, Uruguay.

Foreword

The design and implementation of service trade and investment policies have become high-profile issues for many developing-country governments. Many services are critical inputs in production. The efficiency of the service sectors is an important determinant of the productivity of other industries, whether in manufacturing or agriculture, as well as in other services. Reforms that result in higher quality, lower prices, and greater variety in services are able to generate large welfare gains. However, reforms of service sectors have not always proved successful in attaining social or efficiency objectives. Developing countries face significant difficulties in designing reforms, in part because of concerns about the realization of regulatory objectives.

Service sector policy and regulation are domestic matters. Nonetheless, service policies have effects on the ability of foreign firms to contest markets. The trade in services accounts for over a quarter of global trade flows and has been expanding rapidly in the last two decades because of technological changes. As a result, services are now squarely on the agenda in trade negotiations and trade agreements. Trade negotiations can play a complementary role in promoting beneficial policy reforms, as well as improving market access opportunities for exporters and contributing to the competitiveness and trade diversification strategies of countries. But getting it right is complex—much more so than in the case of the trade in goods—because of the importance of regulation in services. Service regulation is generally sector specific, implying that sectoral regulators and ministries must be part of the negotiating process.

The aim of this book is to help policy makers, especially in the least developed countries, address the complexities of the organization, formulation, and implementation of trade-related reforms in the service sector. The book provides a conceptual framework for trade policy making and negotiation and practical tools that may be used to guide negotiations on policies that affect the trade and investment in services. The aim is not to be prescriptive, but to provide practical recommendations and tools that may be applied in the pursuit of negotiations on services, including consultations and regulatory audits.

Trade policy making in services gives rise to great organizational challenges. Service trade policy making requires the participation of all relevant agencies responsible for trade matters, as well as a comprehensive consultation process wherein all stakeholders may provide their views and suggestions. The long-term sustainability and stability of trade policies depend not only on the design of policies, but also on the implementation of these policies. Both design and implementation are partly determined by the quality of the consultation processes used to build consensus on the way to conduct reforms and manage a more open economy.

Negotiators often have little basic information regarding existing regulations and the purpose of these regulations. This problem is compounded by the difficulty of translating existing regulations into the terminology and concepts used in trade agreements. Different methodological approaches are needed to manage different sets of laws and regulations. This book offers a simple tool to help countries organize information to address these challenges. The book also provides practical examples and negotiation exercises that aim to enhance understanding of ways to use the conceptual framework and related tools.

I hope the material, tools, and practical exercises that are presented in this volume will prove a useful resource for policy makers and negotiators who are engaged in efforts to expand the coverage of trade agreements to trade and investment policies in services.

Bernard Hoekman
Director, International Trade Department
The World Bank

Acknowledgments

This book is the result of the work undertaken by the World Bank's Poverty Reduction and Economic Management Network, International Trade Department. Thanks are due to the following people: Pierre Sauvé (chapter 1), Julio Berlinski (chapter 1, and inputs on aid for trade), Robert M. Stern of the University of Michigan (peer reviewer for chapter 2), Guillermo Arenas, Arti Grover, and Christian Saborowski (chapter 3), and Nora Carina Dihel and Claudia Nassif (peer reviewers of chapter 4) for their valuable comments and suggestions that helped improve the preliminary drafts. In addition, Jean-François Arvis, Norbert Fiess, Pierre Latrille, Charles Kunaka, Jose Guilherme Reis, and Phil Schuler provided valuable comments and ideas on the trade in logistics section (chapter 4). Olivier Cattaneo kindly agreed to include part of his work on health services as background to the respective section of chapter 4. Natalia Ferreira-Coimbra provided valuable collaboration in the development of the database cited in chapter 3 as well as comments and suggestions for a preliminary draft of that chapter. Sebastian Acuña developed the pilot of the services regulation management tool presented in chapter 3.

This project was supported in part by the governments of Finland, Norway, Sweden, and the United Kingdom through the Multidonor Trust Fund for Trade and Development. Finally, the project and the book would not have been possible without the continuous support and guidance of the staff of the International Trade Department and its management team, in particular Mona Haddad and Bernard Hoekman.

The editor would also like to thank Susan Graham, Stephen McGroarty, and Deb Appel-Barker, from the World Bank's Office of the Publisher for their management of the editorial services, design, production, and printing of this book.

Abbreviations

3PL	third-party logistics (supplier)
CARIFORUM	the Caribbean Community (CARICOM) and the Dominican Republic
CPC	United Nations Central Product Classification
GATS	General Agreement on Trade in Services (World Trade Organization)
GATT	General Agreement on Tariffs and Trade
GDP	gross domestic product
NAFTA	North American Free Trade Agreement
PTA	preferential trade agreement
SERET	service regulations management tool
W/120	services sectoral classification list
WTO	World Trade Organization

Note: All dollar amounts are U.S. dollars (US$) unless otherwise indicated.

CHAPTER 1

The Strategic Development Role of Trade in Services

Sebastián Sáez

Trade is normally associated with goods. In the case of goods, trade involves shipping goods from one country to another: crossborder trade. In contrast, in services, trade is possible only via sales through the establishment by the producer of a commercial presence in the country of the customer or if either the customer or producer travels across borders. Usually services are seen as intangible, invisible, and perishable, requiring simultaneous production and consumption.

Service activities have been traditionally analyzed from the point of view of their impact on the competitiveness of countries. The increase in the trade in services has attracted the attention of policy makers in the last 20 years. Changes in technology have allowed the rise in the trade in services in sectors outside traditional activities such as transportation, tourism, and financial services. Within this new service trade, the most important services have been business process outsourcing (offshoring), call centers, software and information technology services, education services, health tourism, and others. In short, services have become a means to diversify the international trade of both goods and services.[1]

Services play a broad and strategic role in the economy. Low-cost, high-quality services generate economy-wide benefits. Financial services, telecommunication services, and transportation services allow a more efficient allocation of resources, are an input in the production of goods and other services, and, through these, contribute to economic growth and the development of countries. Input services facilitate transactions through space (information technology, communication, and logistics services) or time (financial services) (Hoekman and Mattoo 2008, Francois and Hoekman 2009).

The new focus on services arises because services have become increasingly tradable, thereby allowing the emergence of new and improved export activities. The trade in services, particularly business services, has become a dynamic component of trade and an alternative in export diversification for many developing countries. In 2000–2007, before the financial crisis, the trade in services grew as much as the trade in goods, at an average rate of 12 percent. The trade in business services (such as engineering, legal, health, accounting, and management services) grew even more quickly, at 14 percent over the same period. Although developed countries have the lion's share of the trade in services, developing countries have also been able to participate successfully in the trade as service providers. Exports of software and business process services contributed about 33 percent to India's exports and about 7 percent to India's gross domestic product in 2008.

Many developing countries of different sizes and in different regions have been successful at diversifying exports through services. Brazil, Costa Rica, and Uruguay export professional services and services related to information technologies; Mexico exports communication and distribution services; and Chile's distribution and transportation services are among the most important in Latin America. Countries in Africa and in the Middle East and North Africa, such as Kenya, Morocco, South Africa, and Tunisia, provide professional services to Europe. Exports of health services are successfully provided by countries in Asia such as India, the Philippines, and Thailand, as well as by countries in Latin America (Brazil) and the Middle East and North Africa (Tunisia).

Progress in transportation and communication technologies has allowed the fragmentation of production into tasks that may be performed in different locations. The connection among tasks requires an efficient logistics service sector to produce goods. The trade in logistics services provides the connection among tasks performed in different countries. Moreover, the quality of logistics can influence the decisions of firms about which country to locate in, which suppliers to buy from, and which consumer markets to enter (Arvis et al. 2007).

In addition, services play a positive role in development strategies. Ghani (2010) describes the positive correlation among service growth, job creation, poverty reduction, and gender equality in South Asia. All these elements are part of a successful development strategy. Furthermore, the service sector concentrates the most highly educated labor force. These findings tend to confirm the positive impact that a well-conducted reform in the service sector might have on the overall development strategy of countries.

However, service liberalization remains one of the most complex, challenging, and, sometimes, controversial issues in contemporary trade policy. The trade in services often requires the proximity of supplier and consumer. This proximity burden has been weakened by technological progress. Service provision requires a combination of inputs to overcome the proximity burden. Moreover, in certain sectors, the provision of one service requires the joint provision of other services. This is the case of logistics services or tourism services, in which transportation and communication services are critical for a successful industry (Francois and Hoekman 2009).

Unlike the trade in goods, in which liberalization revolves mainly, but not exclusively, around the elimination of tariffs and nontariff barriers at the border, service liberalization requires the elimination of discriminatory barriers that affect services and service providers. Also, service liberalization may require the elimination of nondiscriminatory barriers that restrict trade. In addition, among these latter barriers are nontrade measures aimed at achieving legitimate policy objectives, such as the protection of public order and morals, human life, the environment, access by the poor, safety, and other benefits such as healthy competition and consumer protection, that may unnecessarily restrict trade. The distinction between protectionist objectives and legitimate policy objectives remains a difficult and sensitive issue.

For example, research on Sub-Saharan Africa has shown that, in some countries, if competition is not increased and if road transport services are not successfully liberalized, transport prices will remain high, service quality will not improve, and road users will not reap all the benefits of costly investments in infrastructure rehabilitation (Theravaninthorn and Raballand 2009). In other instances, research has shown that liberalization does not always produce the expected benefits if complementary regulatory measures such as improvements in prudential regulation and competition policies are not implemented (Stiglitz and Charlton 2005, Mattoo and Payton 2007).

Why This Book?

This book aims to address some of the challenges that developing countries, especially the least developed countries, face in the design of policies for the trade in services. It also seeks to provide governments with tools to incorporate services more effectively in export strategies—including negotiations and cooperation with trading partners—and unilateral reform.

One of the challenges addressed in chapter 2 is weak trade policy-making processes. Developing countries must improve the procedures they follow in preparing, adopting, and applying trade policies, including service trade policies.

Confronted with generally weak negotiating, regulatory, and implementation capacities, developing countries are often handicapped in their ability to engage meaningfully in service negotiations. To tackle these disadvantages, a methodology is required to identify key policy challenges faced by developing-country trade negotiators, regulatory policy officials, and service suppliers. A list of questions to which negotiators, regulators, and private and civil society stakeholders, as well as donors, should be directing priority attention with a view to identifying potential negotiating, regulatory, or other policy bottlenecks and helping map an appropriate aid for trade response is necessary in organizing a successful liberalization process (this is covered in greater detail in chapter 2).

The implementation phase of policy reforms and trade agreements requires investments in sounder regulatory regimes and the establishment of enforcement mechanisms to help countries manage more effectively the process of market opening and mitigate any potential downside risks. In making regulations, governments need to take into account a wide range of factors, of which one consideration may be the economy-wide trade and investment impacts of such regulation. The process of liberalizing service markets may require new or different types of regulatory interventions to ensure that important policy objectives continue to be achieved within the new market structures.

A successful strategy requires proper sequencing. In fact, a progressive, orderly, and transparent process allows incumbents to prepare for greater competition, anticipate and mitigate possible distributional downsides, and put in place the proper regulatory framework governing newly competitive market conditions.

Finally, a coherent strategy in services needs to target the real constraints that many developing-country exporters face in attempting to supply newly opened markets. Chief among these are raising quality standards, meeting host country certification requirements, and improving home country trade infrastructure, notably the quality and lowered cost of communication, finance, transportation, and logistics services.

Developing countries face serious resource and administrative constraints on the adequate negotiation of multiple service agreements that will serve their trade interests. The growing importance of the trade in services has translated into the growing prominence of services in trade agreements. Since 1995, all trade agreements involving Japan and the United States have included services. Since the negotiation of the agreements with Mexico in 2000, the European Union has also incorporated services in its negotiations with developing countries, and the trade in services has become an integral part of the Economic Partnership Agreements currently under negotiation by the European Union with the countries of the African, Caribbean, and Pacific group (for example, the Economic Partnership Agreement between the European Community and the countries of the Caribbean Community [CARICOM] and the Dominican Republic [the CARIFORUM grouping] that entered into force in November 2008). Yet, developing countries are often not sufficiently well equipped to negotiate service agreements and implement commitments adequately, particularly in the context of North-South trade agreements. For many developing countries, the administrative burden of handling and negotiating multiple trade agreements has become a serious concern, and this may hamper the opportunities available to these countries to obtain adequate market access for service exports.

Chapter 3 of this book provides the methodology to create a country-specific service agreement database that may be implemented on demand. The book develops in detail the methodological framework for the construction of the database and the core elements that will comprise it, including possible technological platforms.

The basic content of the database includes service sectors, subsectors, and activities committed or received; the type of reservation (market access, national treatment, or other); the mode of supply and the relevant agreements; references to the laws and regulations in which the measures are contained; and descriptions of measures. (Examples to illustrate the content of each item are also provided.) In addition, the classification method used is indicated (the services sectoral classification list [W/120], Central Product Classification equivalence [if any], or the Extended Balance of Payments Services classification, in accordance with the *Manual on Statistics of International Trade in Services* [UN 2002]).

The public service sector in developing countries is characterized by high turnover in human resources, thus requiring constant investment in training efforts. Traditionally, training activities in the service sector focused on three main aspects: (1) trade rules applicable to the trade in services; (2) descriptions of scheduling mechanisms (positive, negative, and hybrid formulas), including writing commitments; and (3) sectoral negotiations in the service area (for example, financial, telecommunication, and maritime sectors) and modes of supply (for example, movements of natural persons). However, little training has been devoted to the organization, preparation, development, assessment, and conclusion of the negotiation process. This training entails simulation exercises that allow negotiators to organize more effectively and understand more accurately the negotiation process and assess the impact of negotiations, including the consultation process within the public sector and the private sector and with representatives of civil society.

The book presents, in chapter 4, a training exercise designed for policy makers, trade negotiators, and trade practitioners working in the area of services. This exercise will help these individuals understand the preparatory and negotiating stages of the process leading to the liberalization of the trade in services. As a framework, the exercise uses the General Agreement on Trade in Services. The choice of this framework reflects the importance of this agreement and its relevance for all developing countries, including countries acceding to the World Trade Organization. Moreover, at the regional level, the General Agreement on Trade in Services model has also been adapted as the framework for liberalization. Finally, the European Union uses the General Agreement on Trade in Services as a framework in its negotiations with developing and least developed countries. Because of these applications, the exercise presented in this book has a wider scope and may be easily adapted to different contexts (bilateral, regional, or multilateral).

Understanding the Strategic Nature of Liberalization

One basic starting point is understanding the meaning of liberalization in the trade in services. First, it means allowing the private sector to participate in the provision of services, and, second, it means allowing foreign providers of services to compete on a nondiscriminatory basis with state-owned companies, if there are any, and with the domestic private sector. Furthermore, trade in services means allowing the provision of services through different modes of supply, that is, crossborder (electronic commerce), consumption abroad (persons traveling abroad to seek medical treatment, for example), commercial presence (or investment), and the mobility of service suppliers.

Alternatively, Francois and Hoekman (2009, 19) define service liberalization as "a reduction in discrimination against foreign suppliers, taking as given (assuming) that the realization of regulatory objectives is not affected."

While the terms *service liberalization* and *service deregulation* are used interchangeably, they mean different things. *Liberalization* means to allow the provision of services by the private sector, to permit foreign ownership and to eliminate restrictions that create incentives for an inefficient and nonoptimal provision of services: a competitive or contestable market. *Deregulation* means the creation of a new regulatory environment that ensures the provision of services in a market-oriented framework, including rules to prevent restrictions on competition.

Service industries are characterized by problems of imperfect and asymmetric information and, in many cases, lack of competition and natural barriers to entry, particularly in sectors with significant network externalities.[2] Problems of imperfect and asymmetric information arise if buyers and service providers face difficulties in assessing the standing of providers (professional services) or consumers (financial services). Therefore, regulation is always necessary in sectors in which market failures are prevalent. To ensure that liberalization provides the expected benefits to consumers and the economy in general, complementary policies that address market failures are required. The key issue is the identification of the best regulatory approach for these services. Restrictions on foreign ownership, on market access, or on the operation of service providers seem to be less effective in addressing market failures. A more effective alternative is to establish a sound regulatory infrastructure. Such an infrastructure should provide for a strong and independent regulator and a timely and effective enforcement mechanism to ensure that regulations are followed and that benefits are captured by the intended economic agents.

Empirical evidence illustrates the strategic importance of services. Francois and Hoekman (2009) review studies that estimate the results of service liberalization. According to the studies, openness is associated with increased export competitiveness in high-technology manufacturing sectors in which services tend to be an important component of total costs. In addition, there is evidence that the increased presence of foreign providers of services following opening is the most robust service variable affecting total factor productivity in manufacturing firms. Moreover, studies also corroborate the positive relationship between service sector openness and growth in developing countries, as well as, in general, a positive dynamic effect from trade liberalization, regulatory reform in services, and growth.

The measurement of the level of protection in services involves a number of complex technical problems. The studies that have been undertaken confirm that, in general, the regime is more open in developed countries than in developing countries. But this is not a uniform result. Developed countries have levels of protection that are similar to the levels in developing countries in sectors such as maritime transportation, air transportation, and, in some cases, professional services. Also, studies confirm differences among developing countries. Thus, the regime is more open in the Latin America and Caribbean region than in other regions, including, in some cases, Eastern Europe and Central Asia. This is also the case if the level of restrictiveness is analyzed from the point of view of the mode of supply. The regimes are more open in the Latin America and Caribbean region and Sub-Saharan Africa than in the countries of the Organisation for Economic Co-operation and Development from the point of view of mode of supply.[3]

Government Regulation and the Service Trade

Service restrictions are, in general, government regulations that are applied to the various modes of service transactions (four modes of supply).[4] Thus, for example, regulations may affect the market access and operations of domestic and foreign suppliers of services equally and, in turn, increase the price or the cost of the services involved. According to Deardoff and Stern (2008), "Service barriers are more akin to nontariff barriers than to tariffs, and their impact will depend on how the government regulation is designed and administered." But barriers are also the consequence of a lack of regulations: for instance, if there is a lack of competition or other market failures.

Regulations may take many forms. They are usually designed to address the specific nature of the service being regulated. Deardorff and Stern (2008) propose two sets of distinctions that tend to apply across many different services and the measures that affect them: (1) regulations that impact entry and rules of establishment versus regulations that impact the operations of firms following their entry or establishment and (2) regulations that are nondiscriminatory versus regulations that are discriminatory (see table 1.1).

Table 1.1   Analytical Structure for the Description of Service Regulations

Discrimination	Entry, establishment	Ongoing operations
Nondiscriminatory	Licensing procedures	Safety, quality, environmental standards, prudential measures in banking
Discriminatory	Nationality or residency requirements	Limitations on operations applicable to foreigners

Sources: Author compilation; Deardorff and Stern 2008.

In the first case, regulations that restrict or impede the establishment of service providers within a market usually reduce the number of providers and therefore the quantity of the supply at any given price. If the regulations affect the ongoing operations of service providers, they increase costs, causing the providers to supply a given quantity only at a higher price. The distinction is useful mainly in classifying different types of barriers.

In the second case, the nondiscriminatory versus discriminatory distinction proposed by Deardorff and Stern determines whether a regulation reduces only the number of foreign providers of services (that is, it is discriminatory) or, instead, raises costs and shifts supply among foreign and domestic suppliers alike. However, a regulation that is nondiscriminatory but impedes the establishment of new service providers will limit trade and competition by favoring providers already established in the market. Therefore, nondiscrimination is not by itself sufficient to absolve a regulation from being protectionist.

Assessing Service Liberalization: A Broader Perspective
What are the main effects of the liberalization of the trade in services? A large portion of the benefits of the liberalization of the service trade derives not from allowing providers to seek better market access abroad, but from the increased competitiveness and efficiency created by the liberalization of the domestic market (Nielson and Taglioni 2004). Thus, international trade not only opens up economic opportunities for developing-country exporters, but also provides access to foreign capital and technology that, through enhanced competition and innovation, may offer consumers more choice in terms of quality and price at home (Cattaneo et al. 2010).

In assessing the liberalization of the trade in services, one must take account not only of the direct gains to consumers and the industries that are users, but also of the impact that liberalization may have on the development of other sectors of interest: for instance, gains in terms of the competitiveness and export of agricultural, manufacturing, or mineral products. Well-regulated and competitive service sectors may lead to a significant boost in the overall competitiveness of economies. In this way, services act as an input that facilitates the trade in goods in general.

Designing a Reform Strategy in Service Liberalization

The reform of restrictive service regulations remains a highly complex issue for which developing countries require significant support. Indeed, in addressing reforms in the service sector, a policy maker requires a set of policy definitions at the domestic level, as follows:

- The desired participation of the state in the service sector and the modality of this participation, that is, as an exclusive service provider; as a service provider in competition with the private sector; by limiting the role of the state to policy designer and regulator, including ensuring competition and enforcement; or a combination of all the above
- The extent of private sector involvement
- The extent of the participation of foreign providers of services
- The regulatory framework that will best serve the objectives of the reforms, including the sequence of reforms

In some sectors, such as financial, telecommunication, and transportation services, the way reforms are adopted and the sequence of the reforms are critical determinants of the final result. In addition, certain regulatory measures that have been in place for a long time must be carefully assessed and possibly replaced by other, more appropriate measures, where these are available. Countries must ensure that a sound sequence of reforms is followed. In other sectors, sequencing may be less relevant, but a sound regulatory framework will nonetheless be required to ensure competition and guarantee public goods such as safety and health.

International experience shows that countries may follow different approaches according to policy goals, level of development, and institutional capacity. However, independently of the direction countries decide to take, certain policies must be implemented to ensure that the sector functions properly, as follows:

- If the state decides to participate directly as a provider, the corporate governance of state-owned enterprises becomes an important issue.
- In addition, a level playing field for all providers must be ensured if competition with the private sector is allowed. In particular, the devel-

opment of the private sector should not be impaired by policies that favor state-owned enterprises.

- A regulatory framework must be implemented to prevent conflicts of interest (if the state is both provider and regulator) or capture. In addition, the separation of functions (policy, ownership, regulation), transparency, and due process are required.
- Regulation to pursue legitimate policy objectives, particularly social policies such as universal access, must be implemented on a nondiscriminatory basis and with a view to avoiding unnecessary barriers to trade.
- To ensure long-term sustainability of the sector, a framework for the design, adoption, and implementation of public policies on the service sector must be established whereby all stakeholders may participate.

The Strategic Role of International Agreements in Services

Because the international tradability of services has increased, countries have incorporated this dimension into their trade policies and trade agreements. Therefore, it is important to understand the positive role that trade agreements play in the context of services. First, such agreements collaborate in the liberalization process if vested national interests oppose liberalization and block initiatives to open access or prevent the establishment of an appropriate regulatory framework. Second, trade agreements create a more stable framework for trade because they are international contracts that may not be changed unilaterally. Therefore, they may also create a path for introducing reforms in a gradual manner and provide rules that cannot be arbitrarily modified. Finally, trade agreements provide political support for the liberalization of the trade in services because they ensure reciprocal market liberalization.

Nonetheless, developing countries should exercise caution. If the liberalization promoted through trade agreements is not adequate, especially from an institutional point of view, this may affect the strength of the domestic regulatory function, especially if the right to regulate—following best international practice—is not adequately preserved. Also, developing countries may assume significant regulatory obligations that may not be appropriate for the reality and level of development of their markets. Finally, trade agreements do not supply the detail required so that a regulatory framework may be established for a well-functioning market. Governments still need to create the regulatory framework necessary to ensure that the benefits of the reforms are captured by all stakeholders. One must keep these basic aspects of liberalization in the service sector in mind in determining the scope of negotiations and addressing in an appropriate manner any downsides to the effects of trade agreements.

The Strategic Nature of Negotiations in the Trade in Services

Countries must also learn how to address their concerns and sensitivities, while preserving policy options. This has been done by developed and developing countries in the context of North-North and North-South negotiations. For instance, in the context of the negotiations on the North American Free Trade Agreement, Canada established a cultural exception, whereby cultural industries were excluded from the service and investment provisions of the agreement. Also, during the negotiations, countries concurred in excluding social services (education, health, and social security services) and measures that favor minority populations from the scope of the service and investment provisions of the agreement. The European Union has also established exceptions in service negotiations. For instance, audiovisual services are not included in the European Union's bilateral trade agreements.

Developing countries may also determine the modes of supply that are to be liberalized. A preferable first step in the liberalization of the trade in services may involve allowing foreign providers of services to establish a commercial presence under the same terms and conditions as nationals. Other modes of supply may be liberalized in later stages. There is some evidence that a positive relationship exists between the existence of crossborder service provision and the existence of the provision of services through commercial presence (Lennon 2007). This means that, in deciding their locations among alternatives, firms assess the investment environment and the ability to provide services through different modes. In developing their negotiating strategies, countries need to be careful to provide a coherent framework consistent with the needs of service providers. A possible option is a gradual liberalization path to prevent short-term market disruptions. For instance, in its negotiations with Canada and the United States on financial services, Mexico designed a mechanism to regulate the pace and characteristics of the opening of the market in the sector.

Developing countries may also establish exceptions on the basis of domestic policy objectives. Developing countries have the strength to negotiate the terms and conditions under which foreign providers may become established within their territories, including any transition period necessary to eliminate market access restrictions or national treatment limitations or any commitment to future liberalization. Developing countries may draw on the many successful (or failed) experiences that are available in developed and developing countries before choosing a specific approach.

International Cooperation as a Complementary Response

Is liberalization of the trade in services enough?[5] Openness in services is not equivalent to export potential in services. There are some puzzling trends in service exports. Developing countries with a high overall restrictiveness index in the service sector seem to outperform other developing countries that have relatively more open regimes. Some developing countries that are not ranked among the most open economies have the most restrictive service regimes or unfriendly business environments and have shown relatively better growth in the export of certain services. Gootiiz and Mattoo (2009) show that restrictive regimes have not deterred Asian countries from becoming successful service exporters. This does not mean that liberalization should not be pursued, but that, by itself, it does not provide sufficient momentum to the performance of service exports. Liberalization does not spontaneously create the entrepreneurial drive, skill endowments, and management capabilities required in exporting services. Complementary policies are needed to ensure that investment in infrastructure and education occurs and that the identification of possible market failures such as information gaps, lack of transparency, and inadequate regulations will be tackled.

The developing countries that have succeeded in exporting services have followed distinct strategies. Some countries have relied on tax incentives and special regimes; some have taken advantage of specific endowments that they found available, such as human skills; and some have followed a wide-ranging liberalization approach. For instance, in Latin America, early reformers, such as Chile and Mexico, have been relatively less successful in the crossborder supply of other commercial services (business and professional services) than developing countries such as Brazil. In fact, in Latin America, the crossborder exports of Chile and Mexico in other commercial services have grown at a less significant rate relative to the corresponding exports in other regions (although both have invested significantly in services abroad). On the other hand, India, which has a high service restrictiveness index and ranks low in the doing business index, is the most attractive global service delivery location according to A. T. Kearney's global services location index (A. T. Kearney 2009).

Identifying the reasons for the success or underperformance of developing countries is a challenge because of the lack of data. The availability of human resources and expertise seems to be a key determinant, however.

Aside from the transport and tourism sectors, countries with better human capital endowments tend to be ranked among the most important exporters of services. Variables such as business environment and financial attractiveness seem to correlate less strongly with service performance. According to Nyahoho (2010), the importance of human capital is clear in exports of computer and information services. Export success in areas such as construction services and public works, royalties and license fees, and computer and information services is positively linked to the intensity of research and development.

Traditionally, the international community has offered special and differential treatment as a means to improve developing-country participation in the world economy.[6] The rationale behind special and differential treatment revolves around the consideration that the least developed countries lack the resources and the institutions to take advantage of the complex rules of the World Trade Organization; so, the offering of preferential access and aid for trade is intended to compensate these countries. Because services are restricted by regulations, the design, implementation, and evaluation of the market access preferences of developed countries are not easy tasks. Moreover, because services vary in nature, this specificity affects the way they may be handled, as well as the development of the related domestic capacity. This is especially the case in the trade in business services (business and professional services, construction, tourism) and the trade in social services (educational, environmental, health, and social services) compared with the trade in infrastructure services (telecommunication, distribution, energy, financial, and transport services), which are mainly intermediary services.

The efforts to install aid for trade and trade facilitation in services involve at least three actions: (1) technical assistance and capacity building to help countries deal with the complexities of service commitments in trade agreements and the provision of training for government officials in the issues involved in commitments and regulations, (2) institutional reform so as to create an institutional and procedural framework for monitoring and evaluating the service trade, and (3) assigning priority to the development of infrastructure services and their role in improving the access of goods, which requires specific investment projects.

Notes

1. See Newfarmer, Shaw, and Walkenhorst (2009) and Lejárraga and Walkenhorst (2009). Mattoo, Stern, and Zanini (2008) provide a comprehensive analysis of

the main relevant issues in the trade in services. See also Copeland and Mattoo (2008) and Deardorff and Stern (2008).

2. Examples of these service sectors are offered by financial, telecommunication, and transportation services.
3. An analysis of service restrictiveness regimes can be found in Gootiiz and Mattoo (2009).
4. This section is based on Copeland and Mattoo (2008) and Deardorff and Stern (2008).
5. Background material for this subsection has been taken from Saéz (2010).
6. Hoekman and Özden (2005) discuss a survey of the experiences with special and differential treatment.

References

Arvis, Jean-François, Monica Alina Mustra, John Panzer, Lauri Ojala, and Tapio Naula. 2007. "Connecting to Compete: Trade Logistics in the Global Economy; The Logistics Performance Index and Its Indicators." Report, World Bank, Washington, DC.

A. T. Kearney. 2009. "Global Services Location Index (GSLI)." Report. http://www.atkearney.com/index.php/Publications/global-services-location-index-gsli-2009-report.html.

Cattaneo, Olivier. 2009. "Tourism as a Strategy to Diversify Exports: Lessons from Mauritius." In Breaking into New Markets: Emerging Lessons for Export Diversification, ed. Richard Newfarmer, William Shaw, and Peter Walkenhorst, 183–96. Washington, DC: World Bank.

Cattaneo, Olivier, Michael Engman, Sebastián Sáez, and Robert M. Stern, eds. 2010. International Trade in Services: New Trends and Opportunities for Developing Countries. Washington, DC: World Bank.

Copeland, Brian, and Aaditya Mattoo. 2008. "The Basic Economics of Services Trade." In A Handbook of International Trade in Services, ed. Aaditya Mattoo, Robert M. Stern, and Gianni Zanini, 84–129. Washington, DC: World Bank; New York: Oxford University Press.

Deardorff, Alan V., and Robert M. Stern. 2008. "Empirical Analysis of Barriers to International Services Transactions and the Consequences of Liberalization." In A Handbook of International Trade in Services, ed. Aaditya Mattoo, Robert M. Stern, and Gianni Zanini, 169–220. Washington, DC: World Bank; New York: Oxford University Press.

Francois, Joseph F., and Bernard Hoekman. 2009. "Services Trade and Policy." Economics Working Paper 2009–03 (March), Department of Economics, Johannes Kepler University, Linz, Austria.

Ghani, Ejaz, ed. 2010. *The Service Revolution in South Asia*. New York: Oxford University Press.

Gootiiz, Batshur, and Aaditya Mattoo. 2009. "Services in Doha: What's on the Table?" Policy Research Working Paper 4903, World Bank, Washington, DC.

Hoekman, Bernard, and Aaditya Mattoo. 2008. "Services Trade and Growth." In *Opening Markets for Trade in Services: Countries and Sectors in Bilateral and WTO Negotiations*, ed. Juan A. Marchetti and Martin Roy, 21–58. Geneva: World Trade Organization; New York: Cambridge University Press.

Hoekman, Bernard, and Caglar Özden. 2005. "Trade Preferences and Differential Treatment of Developing Countries: A Selective Survey." Policy Research Working Paper 3566, World Bank, Washington, DC.

Lejárraga, Iza, and Peter Walkenhorst. 2009. "Fostering Productive Diversification through Tourism." In *Breaking into New Markets: Emerging Lessons for Export Diversification*, ed. Richard Newfarmer, William Shaw, and Peter Walkenhorst, 197–210. Washington, DC: World Bank.

Lennon, Carol. 2007. "Trade in Services: Cross-Border Trade vs. Commercial Presence; Evidence of Complementarity." September, Centre d'Economie de la Sorbonne, Université de Paris 1 and Paris-Jourdan Sciences Economiques, Paris.

Mattoo, Aaditya. 2009. "Exporting Services." In *Breaking into New Markets: Emerging Lessons for Export Diversification*, ed. Richard Newfarmer, William Shaw, and Peter Walkenhorst, 161–82. Washington, DC: World Bank.

Mattoo, Aaditya, and Lucy Payton, eds. 2007. *Services Trade and Development: The Experience of Zambia*. Washington, DC: World Bank.

Mattoo, Aaditya, Robert M. Stern, and Gianni Zanini, eds. 2008. *A Handbook of International Trade in Services*. Washington, DC: World Bank; New York: Oxford University Press.

Newfarmer, Richard, William Shaw, and Peter Walkenhorst, eds. 2009. *Breaking into New Markets: Emerging Lessons for Export Diversification*. Washington, DC: World Bank.

Nordås, Hildegunn Kyvik, and Henk Kox. 2009. "Quantifying Regulatory Barriers to Services Trade." OECD Trade Policy Working Paper 85, Trade Committee, Trade and Agriculture Directorate, Organisation for Economic Co-operation and Development, Paris.

Nyahoho, Emmanuel. 2010. "Determinants of Comparative Advantage in the International Trade of Services: An Empirical Study of the Hecksher-Ohlin Approach." *Global Economy Journal* 10 (1), Article 3.

Sáez, Sebastián. 2010. "The Increasing Importance of Developing Countries in Trade in Services." Prem Notes 152. World Bank, Washington, DC.

Stiglitz, Joseph E., and Andrew Henry Charlton. 2005. *Fair Trade for All: How Trade Can Promote Development*. New York: Oxford University Press.

Te Velde, Dirk Willem. 2005. "Revitalising Services Negotiations at the WTO: Can Technical Assistance Help?" Paper, Overseas Development Institute, London.

Theravaninthorn, Supee, and Gaël Raballand. 2009. *Transport Prices and Costs in Africa: A Review of the Main International Corridors*. Directions in Development Series. Washington, DC: World Bank.

UN (United Nations). 2002. *Manual on Statistics of International Trade in Services*. Statistical Papers, Series M, 86, ST/ESA/STAT/SER.M/86. New York: Statistics Division, Department of Economic and Social Affairs, United Nations.

World Bank. 2009. "Services Trade for Development: The Old and the New." Unpublished paper, International Trade Department, World Bank, Washington, DC.

CHAPTER 2

Negotiating Trade in Services: A Practical Guide for Developing Countries

Mario Marconini and Pierre Sauvé

Introduction

Arguments in favor of open service markets are increasingly being heard worldwide. This applies particularly to key enabling sectors, such as financial services, telecommunications, and transportation, that contribute centrally to a nation's overall economic development. The difficulties of opening service markets to foreign competition are also becoming more evident. Broad and complex policies, regulatory instruments, institutions, and constituencies, domestic and foreign, public and private, are involved. Considerable care must be taken in assessing the nature, pace, and sequencing of regulatory reform and liberalization to enhance a nation's economic growth and development.

Despite the experience gained through more than two decades of bilateral, multilateral, and international negotiations, the trade in services still ranks among the most complex topics in trade diplomacy. The complexity arises from a number of factors, including (1) the intangible nature of service sector activity and the corresponding difficulty of measuring and assessing the sector's contribution to production and exchange and the economic consequences of alternative policy choices,

(2) the considerable diversity of activities in the sector, (3) the challenge of the factor mobility (capital and labor) in service transactions, and (4) the ubiquity (and diversity) of the market failures affecting service transactions and, because of the failures, the intensity of regulatory activity.

The centrality of the intermediation functions of service industries and the consequent impact of services on competitive performance suggest that the benefits of liberalization in the service trade and in investment in services would be far-reaching. Numerous studies have documented the potential magnitude of these benefits, which is typically considered to exceed the magnitude of the benefits emanating from the opening of trade in agricultural and manufacturing products (see Hoekman 2006, Hoekman and Mattoo 2008). However, the benefits of procompetitive reform in service markets have tended to be realized through unilateral efforts at the domestic level rather than through collective action at the negotiating table at the World Trade Organization (WTO) or under preferential trade agreements (PTAs).

The WTO's Doha Development Agenda negotiations have encountered difficulties and have not yet been concluded. Part of the problem can be traced to the fact that the negotiations have focused (perhaps excessively) on trade-offs between agricultural market access and nonagricultural market access. At the same time, there is little doubt that the slow progress in the discussions on services has been caused by the challenges faced by a majority of WTO members in mastering the regulatory intricacies of the service sector and in devising a proper role for services in national development strategies.

Lacking a road map and confronted with generally weak negotiating, regulatory, and implementation capacities, the developing-country members of the WTO are often especially handicapped in their ability to engage meaningfully in service negotiations. The difficulties regularly translate into cautious negotiating stances and levels of bound commitments. The development potential of the service trade and of the negotiations in the sector thereby fails to be properly harnessed. Addressing these various challenges through targeted technical assistance and capacity strengthening must therefore be part of the solution.

Building on the work of Feketekuty (2008), we seek, in this chapter, to provide a practical checklist to help service negotiators, officials in ministries and regulatory agencies, and broad stakeholder communities (including those inside the World Bank and in aid agencies) to gain a better sense of the key moments in the life cycle of service negotiations. These moments might be described as follows:

- *Mapping* a strategy for services in national development plans
- *Preparing* for service negotiations, that is, developing an informed negotiating strategy or identifying the capacity needs required to do so, setting up the proper channels of communication with key stakeholders, and conducting a trade-related regulatory audit
- *Conducting* a service negotiation, that is, acquiring a voice in debates on outstanding rule-making challenges in the service trade by pursuing offensive (as opposed to defensive) interests, devising strategies to deal with defensive concerns, analyzing the negotiating requests of trade partners, formulating one's own requests and offers, and participating in collective requests and offers
- *Implementing* negotiated outcomes, that is, addressing regulatory capacities and weaknesses and identifying implementation bottlenecks
- *Supplying* newly opened markets with competitive services that comply with international standards, that is, addressing the supply-side constraints on the ability to take advantage of the outcome of trade negotiations, including aid for trade in services

The next section focuses on mapping a strategy for services in national development plans. The subsequent section is devoted to preparing for service negotiations; the following section to conducting service negotiations; the section thereafter to enhancing the capacity to supply; and the penultimate section to aid for trade in services. Conclusions are contained in the final section. There are numerous boxes and two tables that provide illustrative examples of the many key points that need to be considered, especially in emerging market economies and in developing countries, in planning, implementing, and evaluating a program of service negotiations.

Mapping a Strategy for Services in National Development Plans

In embarking on service negotiations, governments must clarify the broad policy objectives they wish to achieve at the domestic level. This implies determining the extent to which such agreements are used as an anchor for ongoing policy reforms or as precursors of future reforms, notably through a precommitment to market opening. The purpose is to gain a sense of the likely opportunity costs flowing from various approaches to liberalization and policy bindings under service agreements, including the choice *not* to make new or improved binding commitments, thereby preserving policy space.

The heterogeneity and intangible nature of services pose challenges to service negotiators. Governments tend to consider services in a piecemeal, segmented manner that often reflects the particular characteristics of individual sectors rather than the role of services in the economy. This tendency may be seen in the generally disorganized way in which many governments tackle service issues. Few governments have ministries of services, while most, if not all, have numerous sectoral ministries dealing with individual service sectors. These may include financial services through a ministry of finance or a ministry of the economy, telecommunications services through a ministry of communications (which might also cover postal services, broadcasting, and audiovisual services), a ministry of transportation, and so forth. Many service-related issues also involve more than one ministry or government agency. This is the case in regard to the movement of natural persons and the trade in professional services, which, in many countries, is the shared responsibility of ministries of external relations, justice, education, and immigration.

Developing a clear strategy for services therefore poses, for most governments, genuine institutional challenges in that no single agency takes a holistic view of services and their interlinked contribution to the development and growth process. Accordingly, any attempt to devise a service sector road map or strategic blueprint must start with the establishment of a cross-sectoral, multi-issue steering committee and the designation of a specific ministry, secretariat, agency, or person within the government to carry out a coordinating function, identify the key elements in a service road map, and oversee implementation. The coordination function is not trivial because it cuts across bureaucratic competencies (regulatory turf) and may create tensions between sectoral and economy-wide perspectives.

Considering the economy-wide implications of service sector reform, reform should be coordinated or derive a clear delegation of power from the highest levels of government (for example, the office of the presidency or the prime minister). Sectoral ministries naturally focus on the design and implementation of the policies that are optimal for each sector under their jurisdiction. The establishment of a national development strategy, however, requires that services be thought of in economy-wide terms. Governments should identify growth and development bottlenecks in the economy and direct policy efforts at eliminating the bottlenecks and deciding the role, if any, to be assigned to trade and investment policies in this process. One approach is to address productive chains (activities) or clusters (location) given that these concepts encompass several sectors. This takes into account the interface between services and the industries to which they provide critical inputs, with a view to evaluating the role of service sector policy in the broader context. For instance, if, for a particular supply chain, the main problem is logistics and transportation, this implies a particular set of solutions that involves a range of service sectors. If, in contrast, the main bottleneck is access to imported components, the issue points to trade in goods and the workings of a country's traditional (goods-related) foreign-trade regime. In other instances, the binding constraint may concern the supply of skilled workers, pointing to the need for enhanced efforts in education and training and the possible scope for attracting foreign investment in higher or specialized education services.

With an economy-wide map available, governments are able to prioritize service-related policy responses. In each case, governments must determine if the best solution to a particular problem involves technical support (financial and otherwise), strengthened regulation, enhanced efforts at investment promotion, targeted efforts at trade and investment liberalization, or greater transparency and certainty in domestic policy making.

Unlike other sectors of the economy, services involve a host of national policy objectives, such as prudential regulation, universal access, the preservation of cultural diversity, and the maintenance of high professional standards. These objectives must be clearly defined and factored into the analysis. The boundaries between public and private interests may also have to be properly delineated, especially in the context of the public-private partnerships that are increasingly common in service sectors such as infrastructure and transportation. Finally, the boundary of state sovereignty comes into play in service policy discussions to the extent that service negotiations encompass liberalization in foreign investment. Liberalization in foreign investment includes the possibility of foreign presence and foreign involvement in sensitive sectors.

Any approach to service policy in national development strategies should focus on the pace and manner in which a country wishes to become integrated into the world economy. The revolution in communications and information technologies and the compression in time and distance that has occurred in its wake have transformed the world into a rapidly moving, interconnected community. This can greatly facilitate the scope for plugging into regional or global supply chains, and it allows countries to leapfrog over many technological constraints on development. But it also requires quick responses to emerging social and economic problems. The costs and benefits of opening up and integrating more fully into production networks need to be measured, alongside the cost of *not* opening up or of opening at a different pace or through different means.[1] The effects of various policy choices on employment and restructuring, the possible impacts on national champions, and other strategic considerations must therefore be properly identified and measured.

The checklist in box 2.1 arises from the above considerations with respect to whether, how, and in what manner services and service sector policy (including trade policy in services) are situated in national development strategies.

Box 2.1

The Place of Services in National Development Strategies

- What is the institutional setting for dealing with services within the government?
- Is there an authority, agency, or ministry responsible for coordinating service sector strategies?
- Is the coordinating authority, agency, or ministry capable of making and executing decisions?
- Are services being dealt with adequately from a sectoral perspective? Are there sufficient and well-functioning ministries or agencies devoted to the various services?
- Are services an integral part of the decision-making process in the establishment of national development strategies?
- Are national development strategies based on economy-wide considerations?
- Are the priorities established for the service sector (including the role assigned to trade and investment policy) based on economy-wide considerations, in addition to sector-specific concerns?
- Are distinctions made regarding the horizontal versus sectoral priorities for services?
- Are priorities clear in terms of the support, regulation, or policy making for services and the relationship of services to the overall economy?

(continued)

> **Box 2.1** *(continued)*
>
> • Do specific national policy objectives for services clash with broader objectives for national development?
> • How far should the government intervene in the economic realm in general and in the service sector in particular?
> • Is the service sector sufficiently internationalized? How internationalized should it be according to national development objectives? What role should be assigned to trade and investment policy relative to autonomous liberalization in this regard?
> • Has a cost-benefit analysis been undertaken with respect to the opening up of the economy in general and the opening up of the service economy in particular?
> • Has a cost-benefit analysis been undertaken with respect to the nonliberalization of the economy? How clear are the government and key stakeholders about the opportunity costs of various liberalization scenarios?

Preparing for Service Negotiations

The multiple challenges that the liberalization of the service trade entails should not be underestimated, particularly in light of the limited administrative and negotiating capacities of many developing countries. A government must gather significant knowledge before it is able to submit sensible liberalization requests to key trading partners and make informed market-opening offers. In addition to establishing the proper channels of communication with key stakeholders inside and outside the government, as well as preparing a full inventory of relevant measures to ensure that there is an adequate understanding of the regulatory regime and its possible shortcomings (see below), governments must identify the opportunities and challenges experienced by exporters; determine the capacity-building needs of negotiators, ministries, and regulatory agencies; and assess the likely economic and social impacts of various liberalization scenarios. These are difficult tasks even for developed-country governments, the human and financial resources of which are typically far greater than those of developing countries.

Much of the capacity-building effort in services has tended to focus on helping developing-country negotiators and policy officials master the legal provisions of service agreements such as the General Agreement on

Trade in Services (GATS). For many least developed countries and small and vulnerable economies, as well as a number of countries seeking admission to the WTO, this is an important responsibility, especially because their expertise in trade is relatively weak or is embodied in only a few officials in ministries of trade and foreign affairs. Regulatory agencies and other ministries usually have even less capacity. Short-term training directed at overcoming these knowledge gaps can be useful in many countries, and regional and international organizations are involved in delivering this type of trade-related technical assistance.[2] Regional organizations typically focus their assistance on preferential liberalization initiatives, whereas international organizations (with the exception of the WTO) tend to focus on multilateral and preferential liberalization endeavors.

More pressing needs in trade-related technical assistance are the needs to acquire the analytical tools to determine a country's readiness to liberalize; develop government-wide negotiating strategies; assess the gender, poverty reduction, and human health impacts of service market opening; and help providers of domestic services take full advantage of the market access opportunities arising from regional and multilateral liberalization efforts. Meeting these needs is conducive to harnessing the pro-development potential of service liberalization beyond the GATS and the intricacies of trade agreements covering services. Sustained technical assistance and training efforts directed at these issues have not yet materialized. The issues deserve immediate attention. For the most part, this entails the documentation (in the form of country-, region-, and sector-specific case studies) and dissemination of knowledge on best practices in developed and developing countries. North-South and South-South learning are equally important channels. The diversity of expertise is more easily achieved through international organizations than through bilateral donors in the Organisation for Economic Co-operation and Development.

Negotiating without a Proper Service Road Map
The preparations for international negotiations should occur *after* national development strategies have been established. This is often not the case because countries become involved in negotiating processes without having determined national policy positions. For this reason, many developing countries are not ready politically or administratively to respond to complex regulatory and policy issues that arise in service negotiations. This is particularly the situation if negotiations involve more

mature partner countries that are likely to bargain on the basis of well-informed demands.

In developing countries, international negotiations often become a leading driver of domestic economic reforms, requiring the formulation of policy positions in areas in which a domestic consensus for change has not yet taken root or in which domestic regulatory conditions are insufficiently evolved. Moreover, in many developing countries, an appropriate level of regulation and regulatory capacity has not emerged, although the countries are confronted, in the context of asymmetrical negotiations, with the need to adopt, adapt, update, or reform regulatory regimes. The lack of experience with regulatory reform renders the search for policy responses more difficult. This problem is aggravated by the speed of international negotiations, which usually proceed at a pace that is more rapid than the desirable or feasible pace of domestic political change.

Preparing for international negotiations is thus an exercise in adaptation and approximation. While governments should decide what they want to achieve before they negotiate, there is typically little time for such an assessment. Often, the only option is to identify objectives *during* the negotiating process. These governments must clarify and, eventually, rectify a poor regulatory situation and map out a proper sequence for internal regulatory reform and external liberalization. The position a country takes in negotiations, however, should reflect an equilibrium between the demands of trading partners and what is acceptable based on domestic politics.

Intergovernmental Coordination and Multistakeholder Consultations

In preparing for service negotiations, as in the establishment of a national development strategy in services, an important first step is the creation of a credible, transparent, and efficient coordination process for the negotiations. In trade negotiations, the coordination function often resides with the ministry of foreign affairs, the ministry of trade, or both, and these are also the ministries usually responsible for conducting the negotiations. Intragovernmental coordination is among the most crucial negotiating inputs; it is so important that, alone, it may determine the effectiveness of the country's participation in international negotiations. A government's negotiating position would be severely damaged if different ministries and agencies make contradictory pronouncements about the same negotiating points or if trading partners become confused about the entity responsible for the country's negotiations.

The main objective of coordination is the establishment of a national position on each service-related issue in specific negotiations. A secondary objective is the achievement of consistency and coherence in the management of the external trade environment by the government. Coordinating agencies must master the government's positions across forums and negotiating settings (for example, WTO versus PTAs). In coordinating GATS negotiations, for example, government representatives must be kept mindful of the positions taken and the interests pursued in other negotiating forums so they are able to maintain coherence. This applies to the scheduled commitments governing access to a country's service market, as well as to positions on rules and principles that may vary across agreements or negotiating processes, that is, positive versus negative lists and sectors or disciplines that may be covered in PTAs, but not at the WTO level. Examples include digital trade, e-commerce, and the government procurement of services. Box 2.2 highlights some of the policy-making benefits likely to derive from effective intragovernmental coordination in the service trade.

Box 2.2

The Policy-Making Benefits of Effective Intragovernmental Coordination

Given the regulatory intensity of many service activities and the range of sectors involved, proper coordination across various government agencies is critical. Promoting an effective process of intragovernmental coordination is likely to generate positive policy-making externalities. These include the following.

The creation of a range of government positions. Service negotiations are information intensive. Coordination is essential to the development of negotiating positions based on a thorough assessment of national priorities and to ensuring that negotiators are well informed of all the factors influencing the domestic service market. In countries with federal systems, coordination may also be important in guaranteeing that federal negotiators are adequately prepared in terms of their knowledge and their mandate to address the questions of trading partners about subnational measures.

The creation of an information base on measures affecting the trade in services. A key substantive obligation flowing from most trade agreements covering services is to provide trading partners with accurate information on the domestic

(continued)

Box 2.2 *(continued)*

regulatory environment affecting the trade in services. Meeting this transparency obligation can be assisted through the creation and maintenance of a central inventory or focal point and a database of the various regulatory measures.

The analysis of the effects of measures in helping achieve economic or social policy goals. Governments at all levels must periodically review the effectiveness of domestic policies and regulations in achieving the underlying economic and social policy objectives. This may include an analysis of the trade or investment effects of regulatory measures. Governments must be aware of the impact of service trade disciplines on regulatory conduct in sectors in which commitments are scheduled, including in terms of notification requirements. In developing policy initiatives, all levels of government must take into account current service trade commitments, consider incorporating international standards where applicable, and meet notification requirements and disciplines on regulatory conduct.

The avoidance of duplication in domestic stakeholder and intragovernmental consultations. To retain the cooperation of service firms, especially small service firms, one must avoid unnecessary surveys. If a particular government entity has to consult with the firms under its direct mandate, the consultation should be coordinated with the trade ministry so that the consultation covers any service-related issues, thereby avoiding the need to resurvey the firms about the trade in services.

Given the multitude of subsectors and measures involved in the service trade, it is important to establish a balance between the engagement of intragovernmental partners on issues of mutual concern and avoiding inundating key departments and agencies with too much information or too many requests for input. The establishment of regular lines of communication among individuals may play a significant role in permitting issues to be addressed quickly without creating unnecessary processes.

The maintenance of contributions to ongoing impact assessments of service trade liberalization. In most countries, the data used in impact analyses are the responsibility of the national statistics agency. However, the task is challenging, and the recourse to anecdotal information may be useful. First, service trade agreements address the issue of the flow of services, while data collection is typically focused on populations of service industries. Second, service trade agreements

(continued)

Box 2.2 *(continued)*

cover the four modes of service supply, while data collection is typically focused on crossborder trade (Modes 1 and 4), a limited portion of in-country trade such as tourism or education services (Mode 2), and a little foreign affiliate trade (Mode 3). Third, a particular service may also be exported by goods manufacturers and firms in related service industries; simply surveying a particular service industry may therefore not always offer an accurate picture of export activity. Statistics on the trade in goods cover services that are exported by manufacturers, including services that are bundled with goods (for example, maintenance or training agreements) and stand-alone services sold by manufacturers to foreigners (for example, financial services and consulting services). Bundled services sold to foreigners must be distinguished from domestic service transactions that are embedded in exported goods and, so, are not service exports. It is helpful to alert the various parts of government that participate in data collection to the relevant issues and data requirements in proper assessment.

Source: OECD 2002.

Various options are available to governments in structuring internal policy dialogues and decision-making processes in the service trade. One approach of a number of WTO members is the creation of dedicated working groups in the ministry of trade or commerce to coordinate trade negotiations. Depending on the available resources, a ministry might set up a single group for services or several working groups to cover related service sectors (for example, one group on recreation, sports, entertainment, and tourism; another on transport, distribution, and communications; and so on). Governments with limited resources may focus on creating groups for selected service sectors, although this may raise problems because service sectors are highly interrelated. Working groups might also be considered for issues that are relevant across a range of sectors, such as Mode 4 and labor force development, or opportunities for crossborder trade and e-trade in services. Group participants may self-select based on the relevance of issues to their responsibilities. For example, immigration authorities would have a clear interest in being involved in Mode 4 discussions; telecommunications authorities would have less of an interest.

While governments alone must assume responsibility for carrying out the trade negotiating strategy, the coordination effort must include all key external stakeholders, including the private sector and civil society. The task is challenging because multistakeholder consultations often involve a variety of potentially conflicting interests, ranging from mercantilist export interests to concerns over consumer protection or the preservation of cultural heritage. Although governments sometimes regard the consultative process as unduly onerous and a potential constraint on their decision-making prerogatives, the backing of the key constituencies may be necessary in the ratification and implementation of the negotiated outcomes.[3] Table 2.1 indicates the main private and public stakeholders that might be included in the consultations on various service sectors.

Table 2.1   Sample List of Exporters and Other Domestic Stakeholders in Selected Service Sectors

GATS sector	Exporters	Other stakeholders
Business services	Small and large national firms that sell according to each mode Subsidiaries of transnational corporations (Mode 3) Governmental agencies Nonprofit organizations	Professional service associations Professional licensing registrars Service industry associations Real estate boards Convention boards National research councils Unions
Communication services	As above	Service industry associations Telecommunications regulators National film boards National news services Unions Producers in other sectors that consume the services
Construction and related engineering services	As above	Construction associations Engineering associations Architectural associations Housing authorities Environmental impact agencies Oversight authorities on safety standards Unions Producers in other sectors that consume the services

(continued)

Table 2.1   Sample List of Exporters and Other Domestic Stakeholders in Selected Service Sectors *(continued)*

GATS sector	Exporters	Other stakeholders
Distribution services	As above	Retailer associations Wholesaler associations Importer associations Franchise associations Duty-free shops Unions
Education and training services	As above	Teacher unions Associations of private educational institutions Associations of community colleges Career guidance associations Student associations
Environmental services	As above	Environmental service associations Trade unions Environmental nongovernmental organizations Producers in other sectors that consume the services Consumer groups
Financial services	As above	Banker associations Broker associations Insurance associations Central banks, finance ministries Security exchanges, stock markets Securities regulators Unions Producers in other sectors that consume the services
Health-related services and social services	As above	Hospital associations Outpatient clinic associations Health advocates Social welfare advocates Unions
Recreational, cultural, entertainment, and sporting services	As above	Major sports team managers National museums National libraries and archives National performing arts groups Coalitions of domestic filmmakers Council for the arts Unions

(continued)

Table 2.1   Sample List of Exporters and Other Domestic Stakeholders in Selected Service Sectors *(continued)*

GATS sector	Exporters	Other stakeholders
Tourism and travel-related services	As above	Travel agency associations Tour guide associations Hotel associations Restaurant associations Parks authorities Environmental impact agencies Unions
Transportation services	As above	Airport authorities Air traffic controller associations Port authorities Vehicle licensing authorities Unions Producers in other sectors that consume the services
Other (energy services)	Utility companies Energy trading companies	Utility regulators Industry associations (including in other sectors that consume the services) User, consumer advocates Environmental nongovernmental organizations Unions

Source: OECD 2002.

Effective consultation is an ongoing, two-way process, that is, stakeholders provide initial input and receive initial feedback, then comment on negotiating alternatives, and receive feedback on the negotiations as they progress. If the consultation is only a one-way process, exporter stakeholders may lose interest, and critics or groups with a defensive or rent-protecting agenda may gain disproportionate influence.

Figure 2.1 shows the policy-decision matrix used by the Ministry of Commerce in Thailand to prepare for the various negotiations in which the ministry participates. The matrix reveals the government's recognition that policy decisions must rest on sound analytical inputs and an extensive consultation process within and outside government to ensure that Thailand pursues coordinated and coherent objectives across various negotiating forums.

Public consultations should generally aim to bring together stakeholders with differing views so that individual groups are exposed to all factors

Figure 2.1   Checklist for Trade Policy Formulation, Thailand

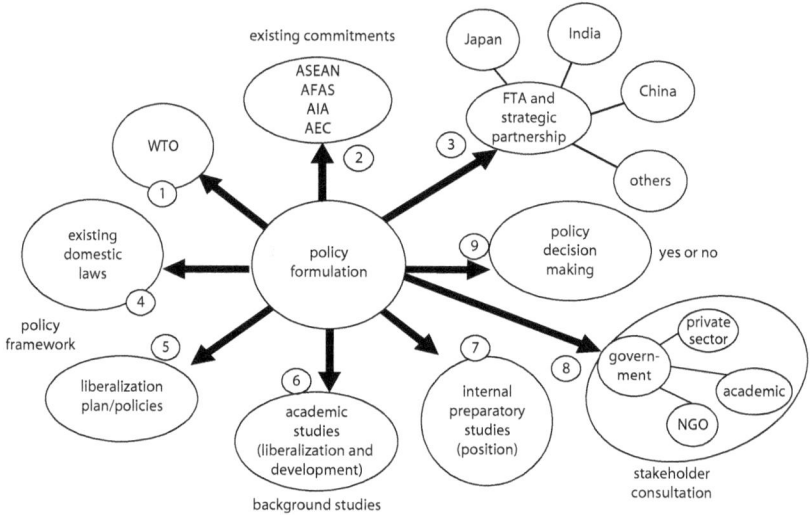

Source: Vonkhorporn 2008.
Note: ASEAN = Association of Southeast Asian Nations. AFAS = ASEAN Framework Agreement on Services.
AIA = ASEAN investment area. AEC = ASEAN Economic Community. FTA = free trade agreement.
NGO = nongovernmental organization.

that the government must take into account and balance in the negotiating process. It may also be helpful to confront domestic service exporters with the interests of consumers, producers, service importers, and public interest groups in public debates. The economic and political consequences of trade and investment liberalization in the service trade and the related regulatory reform issues should thereby be clarified. Such debates may help address misunderstandings in the public policy discourse over liberalization and reform issues.

The mix of stakeholders should therefore be broad and representative, even though this may make debate more controversial. The mix may also have to show a balance between the subnational and the national, depending on the weight of institutions in each case. A balance must also be realized between institutions that are more horizontal (for example, a chamber of commerce representing several sectoral interests) and institutions that are more narrowly sectoral (for example, a banking federation or professional service associations). However, as in government, it is still relatively rare for the private sector, particularly in developing countries, to be organized around all-inclusive coalitions or other types of groups dealing with services. Given the key intermediary role many services play throughout the economy, it will be helpful to reach out to consumer communities (including in the agricultural, mining, and manufacturing sectors) rather than focusing solely on the negotiating preferences of service producers.[4] Building up the capacity of consumer advocacy organizations or supporting the creation of such organizations may be useful in promoting procompetitive, consumer-friendly outcomes in policy design.

An especially sensitive issue is the balance to be struck in consultations among business associations, trade unions, and nongovernmental actors (including nongovernmental organizations). Nongovernmental actors, in particular, tend to take vocal positions on significant trade issues in services, often question the benefits of liberalization, and caution against the liberalization of services that provide public goods such as education, health care, water distribution, cultural industries, and others.

Drawing on the experience of Thailand's Ministry of Commerce, figure 2.2 illustrates the sorts of interagency and external stakeholder consultations needed to make service negotiations successful.

Figure 2.2   Negotiating Essentials: Interagency Coordination and External Stakeholder Consultations

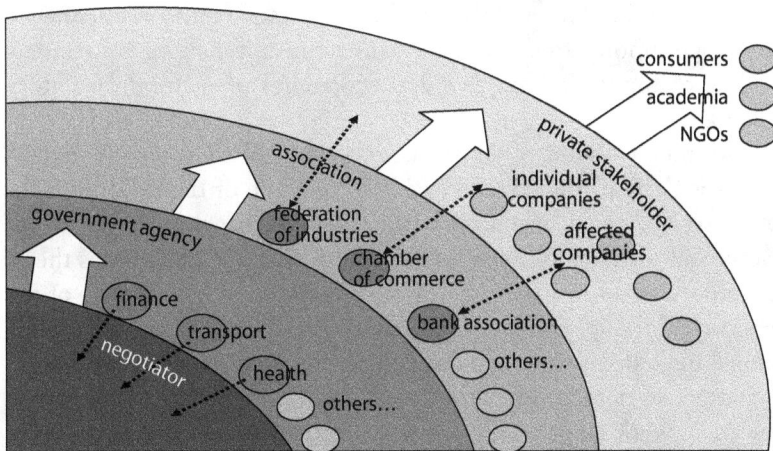

Source: Vonkhorporn 2008.
Note: NGOs = nongovernmental organizations.

Conducting a Trade-Related Regulatory Audit

Because the currency of service negotiations is domestic regulation, much of the preparatory work must focus on the domestic regulatory regime and its relevance in a trade policy context: how it is framed, what objectives are pursued and with what degree of efficiency, whether domestic regulatory requirements are rooted in international standards or international best practice, whether domestic rules and administrative procedures are user-friendly, how and by whom domestic regulations are applied, whether domestic regulatory regimes are trade- and investment-friendly, and whether domestic regulatory objectives can be attained in ways that are less restrictive on trade and investment.[5]

An inventory audit of domestic regulatory measures affecting services and the trade in services should be compiled on the basis of existing legislation and regulations. This internal exercise strengthens interagency coordination and promotes a healthy dialogue among the officials involved in domestic and external policy matters, while also favoring a culture of regulatory reform and regulatory impact assessment. Thus, a trade-related audit may be useful even in the absence of international negotiations.

Trade and investment negotiations offer excellent opportunities for engaging in such an exercise. This, in turn, helps to address the need for investments in trade-related capacity among regulatory officials who may have limited knowledge or experience of international agreements, trade law, and negotiating processes. It may also enhance knowledge among trade officials who may not have a full understanding of the underlying law and economics of sectoral regulatory challenges.

Performing an audit of all service-related regulations may be daunting, particularly if the exercise exceeds the scope of the measures subject to service trade negotiations (box 2.3). Enhancing the ability of government officials to gain a fuller understanding of trade law is therefore important for properly identifying and describing the nature of the domestic regulatory conduct that may be expected to arise from international trade discussions and distinguish this from more purely domestic matters of nondiscriminatory conduct. Regulatory officials tend to view their work as primarily domestic. Yet, the advent of trade disciplines on services in the GATS and in PTAs has revealed that much of what regulators consider domestic lies within the perimeter of trade and investment negotiations.

Box 2.3

Performing a Trade-Related Regulatory Audit in Services

The two-way interaction afforded by the request-offer process on which service negotiations typically rest can be useful if it underpins attempts to benchmark a country's domestic service regulations with the regulations of the country's main trading partners and if it identifies the means to achieve greater policy convergence or shifts toward best (often procompetitive) regulatory practices. This benchmarking and the related need (in response to requests from trading partners) to identify more precisely the policies and measures that may or may not be addressed in the negotiations may also allow a useful policy dialogue to take place among trade officials, sectoral regulators, and officials in other government agencies and departments, as well as key stakeholders in business and civil society. Such two-way policy interaction may also be an important means of answering the central issue of the policy objectives developing countries ultimately wish to pursue in their GATS and PTA negotiations domestically and in foreign markets. The questions that may arise in a domestic dialogue aimed at informing the request-offer process include the following:

- What is the policy objective pursued by the relevant regulatory measure?
- Is the policy objective pursued by the specific measure consistent with overall government policy?
- How transparent is the regulatory measure and the process to adopt it?
- Are private sector stakeholders, domestic and foreign, consulted prior to the enactment of new policy measures?
- When was the policy measure, law, or regulation enacted?
- When was the measure last invoked?
- Is the measure periodically reviewed?
- Is the government satisfied that the policy objective is being achieved, and has it developed a framework to assess the effectiveness of the regulatory regime?
- Can the policy measure be achieved through other means or in a manner that might lessen the restrictive impact on trade or investment?

Performing an audit of a country's regulatory regime in the context of negotiations on the service trade and investment liberalization may thus generate positive policy spillovers in domestic regulatory conduct and design and contribute to strengthening the consultations within and outside the government on services.

(continued)

Box 2.3 *(continued)*

Among the reasons governments might be interested in engaging in a trade-related regulatory audit are the following:

- Ensuring that key regulatory objectives are met in the most efficient manner (that is, in the manner that is least wasteful of scarce public resources), including prudential, consumer protection, or social policy objectives
- Identifying antiquated or inefficient regulations and adopting or converging toward international best practices; in financial services, for instance, this may allow the benchmarking of the degree to which domestic prudential standards and regulations approximate agreed international norms such as the norms of the Bank for International Settlements, the International Organization of Securities Commissions, and the International Association of Insurance Supervisors
- Encouraging, where feasible, the adoption of regulations that facilitate market access (procompetitive)
- Building trust within the government (that is, encouraging a whole-government approach to domestic regulation) through dialogue among trade negotiators, ministries, and sectoral regulators
- Deepening dialogue with key external stakeholders, including local and regional governments; producers, users, and consumers; nongovernmental organizations; and the academic community; in some cases, gaining a better understanding of the reasons for the need to maintain potentially trade- and investment-restrictive measures

A useful starting point for such an audit is the preparation of a list of nonconforming measures—that is, the equivalent of a negative list of measures, which, absent their inscription in reservation lists, would breach the key liberalizing provisions in trade agreements (national treatment, market access [quantitative restrictions], local presence requirements, and most favored nation treatment)—and to describe comprehensively (1) the sectoral nature of the listed nonconforming measures (for definitional purposes), (2) the level of government at which these measures are applied (that is, municipal, subnational, or national), (3) the legal anchoring of the measures (that is, the full citation of the relevant law or regulation), and (4) the precise nature of the nonconformity of the measures.[a]

These audits were pioneered during the preparation of the negative lists of nonconforming measures defining the legally binding commitments of the

(continued)

Box 2.3 *(continued)*

parties under the North American Free Trade Agreement.[b] A trade-related regulatory audit may be put to several uses, as follows:

- The provision of a comprehensive overview of the trade- and investment-restrictive components of a country's regulatory regime
- The identification of regulations needing reform or elimination (which may then yield useful negotiating currency)
- The confirmation of the legitimacy of trade- or investment-restrictive regulations
- The addition of greater clarity to the hierarchy of trade- and investment-restrictive measures (for example, understanding the type of restrictive measure that is most likely to be considered by trading partners as unfriendly to market access); this may encompass nondiscriminatory measures, particularly quantitative restrictions (that is, market access measures), including prudential measures
- The identification of measures that may be scheduled in trade agreements (that is, in making new or improved negotiating offers)
- The anticipation of negotiating requests by partner countries and the assessment of the scope for opening up, reforming, or not altering regulations

The negative list–based regulatory audit depicted above focuses policy attention on measures that are either overtly discriminatory (in the case of measures violating the national treatment and most favored nation provisions of trade agreements) or that overtly constrain the level of market competition allowed (in the case of market access or nondiscriminatory quantitative restrictions).

A trade-related regulatory audit conducted along these lines may not provide a full reading of all nondiscriminatory measures that are unduly burdensome or that act as disguised restrictions on trade and investment and for which trade disciplines are being sought under the GATS article VI:4 work program. Identifying such measures is inherently more difficult and requires considerably more dialogue among trade negotiators, ministries, and sectoral regulators and greater technical competence than the expertise available in many trade ministries.

Despite these caveats, a trade-related regulatory audit that maps restrictive governmental measures affecting trade and investment in services can yield important gains in transparency and help anticipate the red lines in negotiations and bottlenecks in implementation.[c] The technical homework and regulatory dialogue that flow from such an exercise can also promote a culture of

(continued)

Box 2.3 *(continued)*

procompetitive regulatory reform. Conducting an audit is a useful means to prepare for service negotiations, to master the sectoral intricacies and the technical details that are the currency of service negotiations conducted along request-offer lines, to give service providers a one-stop inventory of the restrictive measures maintained at home (and in the markets of key trading partners to the extent that such efforts are reciprocated or mandated by trade agreements), and to afford negotiators a complete road map of measures to target and prioritize in negotiations. None of the above is readily achievable without precise information on the regulatory status quo.

Source: Sauvé 2008.

a. In the Canadian context, the compilation of the list of nonconforming measures maintained at the federal level was carried out over four months by a small group of young officials chosen for their expertise in law. The group was under the supervision of a member of the service negotiating team. The supervisor provided the group with a methodology to produce comparable reservations across all service sectors. Once the inventory was completed in draft form, the trade negotiating team met with ministries and sectoral regulatory agencies. The team asked them to verify the accuracy of the information that had been collated. Then, during a second phase, it engaged in a policy dialogue on the rationale behind the restrictive measures identified, the possibility (or not) of achieving these objectives through other means (including through nondiscriminatory measures), and the scope for removing (or not) the nonconforming measures or progressively reducing the level of nonconformity within the context of the negotiations on the North American Free Trade Agreement. A similar dialogue was carried out with private sector representatives, who were asked about the scope for modifying or eliminating the restrictive measures maintained at the domestic level.

b. Such lists of nonconforming measures are found in PTAs that are modeled on the North American Free Trade Agreement and that pursue a negative list–based approach to liberalization. A number of more recent PTAs, notably those negotiated by Japan, have sought to embed negative lists solely for transparency purposes. In this case, the legally binding commitments on services of the respective parties are governed by the hybrid scheduling approach found in the GATS. This approach adds the voluntary, positive selection of sectors, subsectors, and modes of supply used to schedule the commitments to the negative listing of limitations to national treatment and market access maintained in scheduled sectors, subsectors and modes of supply. Unlike the GATS, in which parties are free to determine the level of their positive bindings, the Japanese PTAs feature an obligation to lock positively listed commitments into the regulatory status quo. This approach has been replicated, most recently, in the Economic Partnership Agreement entered into by the member states of the European Community and the countries of the Caribbean Community (CARICOM) and the Dominican Republic (the CARIFORUM grouping) (see box 2.15).

c. The red lines are the points beyond which negotiators are not prepared to engage or commit.

Box 2.4 provides concrete illustrations of the information a regulatory trade audit typically generates. The list closely tracks the information required to produce a negative list of nonconforming trade and investment measures.

Box 2.4

Illustrative Examples of Trade-Related Regulatory Audits

1. Singapore–United States Free Trade Agreement: Singapore's schedule
Sector: Financial services
Subsector: Banking services
Type of reservation: Market access and national treatment
Level of government: National
Measures: Banking Act, Cap. 19; MAS Notice 619 (Singapore)
Description: Only a maximum of 20 new wholesale bank licenses will be granted by the Monetary Authority of Singapore between June 30, 2001 and June 30, 2003. Quantitative limits on the number of wholesale bank licenses will be removed for U.S. banks three years after the date of entry into force of the agreement. Wholesale banks are not permitted to (a) accept fixed deposits in Singapore dollars of less than S$250,000; (b) offer savings accounts; (c) operate interest-bearing current accounts in Singapore dollars for natural persons who are Singapore residents; (d) issue bonds and negotiable certificates of deposit in Singapore dollars unless the requirements pertaining to the minimum maturity period, the minimum denomination, or the class of investors contained in the Guidelines for Operation of Wholesale Banks issued by the Monetary Authority of Singapore are complied with.

2. Japan-Philippines Economic Partnership Agreement: Japan's schedule
Sector: Financial services
Subsector: Banking services
Industry classification: JSIC 612 (banks, except the Central Bank); 621 (financial institutions for small businesses)
Type of reservation: Market access and national treatment
Level of government: Central government
Measures: Deposit insurance law (Law No. 34 of 1971), article 2 (Japan)
Description: The deposit insurance system only covers financial institutions that have head offices within the jurisdiction of Japan.

3. North American Free Trade Agreement: Mexico's reservation list (annex I)
Sector: Communications
Subsector: Entertainment services (cinema)
Industry classification: CMAP 941103-private exhibition of films

(continued)

Box 2.4 *(continued)*

Type of reservation: National treatment (article 1202); performance requirements (article 1106)
Level of government: Federal
Measures: Ley de la Industria Cinematográfica; Reglamento de la Ley de la Industria Cinematográfica (Mexico)
Description: Thirty percent of the screen time of every theater, assessed on an annual basis, may be reserved for films produced by Mexican persons residing either within or outside the territory of Mexico.

Governments responsible for coordinating the preparatory work for negotiations should aim to gather an inventory of measures that will enable them to seek answers to at least a few basic policy issues, as follows:

• Whether the existing regulation or regulatory regime is adequate and acceptable or whether it needs changing
• Whether changes may be contemplated within the time frame of ongoing international negotiations
• Whether regulatory changes may be offered in international negotiations

These elements are important for several reasons. First, offers in service negotiations may require the binding of existing regulatory situations, and countries should avoid scheduling legally binding measures that domestic regulators do not find adequate or fully developed. Second, the changes in domestic regulations that may be needed or that may be contemplated for internal or domestic political reasons may constitute valuable offers in the negotiations if they tend to improve on the conditions for market access or national treatment. It makes sense to promote formal changes and offer them while there is still an opportunity to obtain reciprocal concessions from major trading partners.

Box 2.5 indicates some of the key questions that arise during the preparatory phase of service negotiations.

Box 2.5

Key Questions during the Preparatory Phase of Service Negotiations

- Is there a sectoral or national development strategy for services that should be taken into account during the preparations for negotiations?
- Has thought been given to the place of reform in the development of the domestic service market and the relationship of reform to the international trade negotiations at hand?
- Is the coordinating authority, agency, or ministry in place and ready to operate?
- Have capacity-building needs been identified with respect to the overall approach to liberalization and trade agreements, that is, the readiness to liberalize, the strategies to be adopted in negotiating liberalization, and the advantages to be obtained from negotiations, particularly in terms of access to foreign markets?
- Are the other external priorities in related international forums clear to all participants in the preparatory process, for example, the positions and commitments taken in the context of bilateral agreements?
- Is there a reasonable understanding among those participating and, in particular, within the coordinating entity on the measures in international trade agreements that affect the trade in services?
- Do those coordinating the work need more capacity building in matters relating to international trade agreements?
- In the case of sectoral ministries and agencies, what is the most effective way to pursue the capacity-building exercise?
- Does an inventory of the measures affecting the trade in services already exist at the horizontal or sectoral level? Beyond its use in trade negotiations, is the information gathered in such inventories being used to underpin a domestic dialogue with key regulatory agencies and external stakeholders and to promote regulatory review and reform processes?
- Once an inventory of regulatory measures has been carried out, what is the basis for determining whether regulatory requirements are adequate, acceptable, or in need of change?
- In instances in which regulatory changes appear necessary, can or should the changes be contemplated within the time frame of ongoing international negotiations?

(continued)

Box 2.5 *(continued)*

- If so, could or should these changes be presented as part of the offer the country is making in the negotiations?
- In the case of all measures, what are the criteria for choosing the measures to be applied, the modes of supply, and the sectors to be offered as bound, partially bound, or unbound in the negotiations?
- Has a clear distinction been established between defensive and offensive interests in the negotiations? How does the government establish the red lines for its negotiators?
- Are offensive interests able to take advantage of the negotiations, or is there a need for additional capacity building, particularly in private sector supply?
- Have studies on the export market been conducted within the government or by the private sector?
- Has all relevant information (public, private, international, and so on) on export interests been compiled, analyzed, and circulated among participants in the preparations?
- How significant are the voices of consumer and user groups in the formulation of service sector policy? Should technical assistance be directed at nurturing or sustaining the development of these voices?
- Has the coordinating entity managed to organize the necessary consultative process with all relevant stakeholders in the public and private sectors, including trade unions and nongovernmental organizations?
- Is the consultation process with stakeholders sufficiently broad to be representative?
- Does the decision-making process seek to achieve a balance among sectoral, individual corporate, and economy-wide objectives (both offensive and defensive)?

Conducting Service Negotiations

Service negotiations tend to be complex affairs, as are the sectors involved. A first concern of governments in conducting service negotiations is to organize a coordinated approach to the talks and identify key issues that require attention early. Because service negotiations involve important, but highly heterogeneous sectors, the composition of the delegations for negotiations is crucial. This is especially true given the budgetary constraints most developing countries face. Thus, because sector-specific expertise cannot be maintained in Geneva, there must be minute monitoring of the negotiating process and a competent means of communicating information to capital cities to keep the relevant officials updated so they may intervene.

Service negotiations essentially involve the mastery of two key issues, rule making and market opening, both of which (especially market opening) must be based on constant coordination and consultation with key stakeholders inside and outside government.

Making Rules for the Service Trade

The initial emphasis in service negotiations is often on rule making, a phase of negotiations that may encompass diverse issues, old and new. These typically range from the approach in scheduling commitments (that is, a top-down approach using a negative list, a bottom-up approach using a hybrid list, or a combination of the two) to questions of scope and definition and to the unfinished rule-making agenda of the GATS (that is, domestic regulation, emergency safeguards, government procurement, and subsidies), which is, for the most part, an unmet challenge in PTAs as well.

Rule-making discussions also typically feature frontier issues, including whether and how to address e-commerce and digital trade in service negotiations; whether and how to address cultural cooperation (with or without legally binding commitments to market access); whether and how to ring-fence sectors, such as public health and education, in which concerns about specific items related to public goods may predominate; the need to design procompetitive regulatory provisions to open up trade and investment in network industries; the need for competition policy complements to market opening in sectors prone to market dominance and anticompetitive conduct; the specific treatment of investment in service industries (a central challenge in PTAs featuring comprehensive investment chapters); how best to enhance the treatment of labor mobility; agreeing on operational modalities for aid for trade in services; and so on.

Many developing-country governments regard themselves essentially as rule-takers in trade negotiations, including in services. They thus take a relatively passive stance in discussions on rule-making issues. This tendency may be more pronounced at the PTA level, particularly if the negotiations are conducted along North-South lines and if developed-country governments, as often occurs, come to the negotiating table with a predetermined platform of rules and substantive obligations and only limited scope for negotiation, modification, and innovation.

Yet, while the negotiating asymmetries are an unfortunate fact of life in trade diplomacy, developing countries have a major stake in crafting the rules governing the service trade. For this reason, they need to exhibit a proactive stance in talks and strive to identify, formulate, and defend their proposals in areas of priority interest. At the WTO level, as well as in regional negotiations, they must also reach out more to other developing countries to pool scarce negotiating resources and build coalitions to support specific issues (particularly Mode 4 trade, e-commerce and crossborder supply, emergency safeguards, and special and differential treatment).

Developing countries should participate especially in the discussions on the interface between domestic regulation and external liberalization, the GATS article VI:4 work program. This is so because strengthened regulatory disciplines may promote sounder governance and greater transparency in domestic markets, with the attendant signaling externalities. Stronger disciplines in domestic regulation can also provide an effective means of challenging the regulatory practices in foreign markets that are needlessly burdensome or serve as disguised restrictions on trade.

Technical assistance and efforts in capacity building targeted at helping developing-country negotiators acquire a greater voice in service rule making may be particularly useful. The broad pool of former service negotiators, particularly in leading developing countries, should be harnessed to this end. This might be accomplished through the establishment of a roster of experts that the World Bank or regional development banks could administer. Developing-country governments might also outsource part or all of the crafting of rule-making proposals to nongovernmental and policy research organizations that have developed considerable technical expertise in services.

Opening Service Markets

While the rule-making agenda in services remains significant and is important to all members of the trade community, much of the attention in service negotiations is devoted to market opening and specific liberalization commitments.

Unlike discussions on nonagricultural market access or on agriculture, service negotiations have largely eschewed formulas (linear or nonlinear), coefficients, and thresholds for negotiations (box 2.6). This reflects the difficulty of quantifying nontariff (that is, regulatory) barriers to trade and investment. Absent formula-based approaches, governments continue to

Box 2.6

The Doha Round Shift toward Collective Requests

For lack of a credible alternative and drawing on mercantilist reflexes honed in goods (that is, tariff) negotiations, the bilateral request-offer approach was adopted in the Uruguay Round as the dominant negotiating method for opening up service markets.[a]

Concern over the limited progress, time-consuming nature, and information-intensive asymmetries implicit in this approach led to a decision by the trade ministers at the December 2005 WTO ministerial meeting in Hong Kong, China to supplement, where practicable, bilateral request-offer discussions by plurilateral negotiations, the results of which would then be extended to all WTO members on a most favored nation basis. This approach involves groups of WTO members—akin to the numerous "friends groups" already existing under the GATS—that propose negotiating objectives in a sector or a cluster of sectors.

At first, the shift toward plurilateral (or collective) discussions revealed a paradoxical aversion of developing countries toward alternatives to the current bilateral approach, even though the bilateral approach is more taxing on developing countries than on developed countries. This is mainly because of the considerable resources and time required by bilateral request-offer discussions, the limited number of service experts available for bilateral discussions in Geneva and in capital cities, the negotiating imbalances that flow from the limited ability of most developing countries to formulate their own requests, the significant asymmetries in the information relevant to negotiations that is available to policy officials, and the more limited stakeholder consultations, private sector engagement, and presence abroad of service suppliers. All these factors tend to interact to produce least common denominator, precaution-induced outcomes at the negotiating table. This complicates attempts to marshal corporate interest in multilateral negotiations and tends to shift incentives toward bilateral or neighborhood responses through PTAs.

Plurilateral approaches are likely to economize on the scarcest commodities—time and human resources—and afford developing countries significant economies of scale in negotiating efforts. Avoiding the sector-by-sector and country-by-country bartering of commitments may substantially reduce the transaction costs of negotiations. These approaches also offer a useful means for developing countries to pool their resources in pursuit of common objectives and join forces with other country groupings (developed and developing) to help build useful reform coalitions in talks.

(continued)

conduct negotiations by focusing on the exchange of commitments on market access and national treatment on the basis of sectors and modes of supply, with occasional reliance on GATS article XVIII (additional commitments). This article relates to precommitting or phasing in future market opening, allowing for a smoother transition to greater market openness, and the related structural adjustment challenges.

Opening service markets typically involves many policy parameters and layers of impediments, some of which may be overlapping. Many of these impediments are narrowly sectoral and relate to a host of regulatory measures that may affect the quality and certainty of the access to and presence in service markets. Many other policy parameters may not be sector specific, but relate to more generic or horizontal policy measures (for example, investment and labor mobility). Still other policy measures may lie wholly outside what is often considered the central focus of service negotiations (for example, issues related to standards, competition policy, and access to government procurement markets).

An important question confronting governments in request-offer negotiations concerns the level of ambition in the scheduling of legally binding commitments under service agreements. The choice of what to make binding is likely to have important implications for domestic economic performance and regulatory conduct. For instance, the impact of de novo liberalization on competition (that is, implying the elimination or progressive reduction of *existing* restrictions to trade or investment in services), the response of foreign direct investors, domestic incumbents, employment levels, and the design of domestic regulatory regimes is likely to differ significantly from the potential impact flowing from a decision to bind the regulatory status quo (that is, freezing the current level of policy restrictiveness) or to bind at a level below the regulatory status quo (which the GATS and GATS-like agreements allow).

In deciding the type of access to request or offer, a government must typically address three core issues: the benefits to be achieved, the political concerns and downsides, and the required regulatory framework or regulatory reform efforts. Table 2.2 lists important policy considerations likely to influence the formulation of negotiating requests and offers. Given the perceived shortcomings in regulatory regimes and external competitiveness, developing countries tend to focus negotiating energy on defensive interests, that is, the protection of the home market from foreign competition through limited offers on market opening. This generates a cost in unrealized offensive interests in terms of key export markets. One reason for this negotiating stance lies in the pronounced asymmetries in service negotiations arising because of the capacity and informational deficits that are often more substantial in poorer countries.[6] These deficits revolve around the genuine difficulties most developing country governments experience in collecting information on the regulatory barriers that are maintained in foreign markets and that hamper the growth of home-country suppliers. A second reason for the negotiating stance stems from the sensitivities in offering foreign interests enhanced access to a home market or in allowing foreign services and foreign suppliers of services an equal regulatory footing with domestic competitors. A third reason for defensive posturing resides in the difficult demands that developed countries often make at the negotiating table, forcing their negotiating partners to focus on the responses. A fourth reason is the fact that offer lists deal with host-country regulations. In this case, precision is an imperative because governments are keen to avoid situations in which imprecise offers (and, thus, prospective commitments) sow the seeds of future trade disputes, demands for compensation, or retaliatory measures. The informational deficits that burden developing-country governments during service negotiations aggravate these problems and reinforce the tendency of these countries to exhibit considerable precaution in undertaking new or enhanced commitments in the service trade.

Despite these challenges, the past few years have witnessed a sea change in the level of engagement by developing countries in service negotiations across sectors. This new landscape attests to the growing realization that developing countries possess comparative advantages in the supply of many services, particularly services that make intensive use of labor.[7] It also attests to the widening agreement that the offers in negotiations help secure enhanced access to imports (including imports of capital), particularly imports of key infrastructural services, and the economy-wide benefits likely to derive from such access. As in the case

Table 2.2 Factors to Consider in Formulating a Request or Offer

Group	Possible benefits	Concerns to be addressed, including through regulatory reform
Country, economy in general	• More efficient use of resources • More foreign investment attracted • Expanded job opportunities, reduced drain on human resources • Enhanced labor force skills • Increased foreign exchange earnings • Increased tax revenues • Economic diversification • Increased service efficiency • Increased technology transfer • Increased economic growth throughout the economy	• Determine the impact on domestic economic performance and the regulatory conduct of various levels of policy binding (for example, below the status quo, status quo, precommitment to future liberalization) • Ensure quality services • Ensure adequate infrastructure for business activities • Assess the impact of market opening on the scope for achieving universal service supply and access objectives, particularly for the poor and geographically disadvantaged • Improve environmental stewardship and address the possible adverse environmental impacts arising from liberalization • Ensure the ability to regulate according to the best international practices where feasible and enforce regulatory regimes adequately • Restrict the scope for illegal activities • Maintain a stable political and economic environment • Maintain adequate means to discipline the potential anticompetitive conduct of dominant firms (domestic and foreign) • Assess whether competition policy can play a larger role in disciplining market conduct after liberalization? • Ensure adequate tax revenue for the government • Ensure adequate resources to address labor force retraining needs, particularly among employees in state-owned enterprises

Consumers	• Lower prices for services (leading to a higher standard of living, greater purchasing power) • Higher-quality service (including convenience, responsiveness, timeliness) • Greater choice, new service offerings	• Assess the impact of market opening on the scope for achieving universal service supply and access objectives, particularly for the poor and geographically disadvantaged • Ensure the adequacy, reliability, and quality of public services • Safeguard consumer rights and provide a redress for complaints • Ensure sensitivity to local needs
Business services	• Lower costs of doing business, increased profitability • Ready availability of capital, reduced cost of funds • Greater ability to own and dispose of assets • Fewer foreign exchange limits, greater ability to repatriate profits • Infusion of new technologies and innovation • Greater adherence to international standards • Enhanced scope for mergers and strategic alliances • Remove red tape, increase transparency of domestic regulatory requirements • Access to skilled labor and expertise (locally and abroad) • Access to larger markets • Access to cheaper service inputs, thereby increasing efficiency and competitiveness	• Allow local firms to recoup initial investments • Encourage reinvestment in improved services • Ensure the growth of local enterprises • Ensure the acceptance of locally produced services • Encourage the adoption of and compliance with international standards • Ensure the availability of appropriately skilled workers • Ensure the disclosure of financial information by foreign firms • Ensure financing at competitive rates • Ensure effective professional (service industry) associations

Source: OECD 2002.

of the trade in goods, the principal gains from the trade in services—those most likely to enhance national welfare—relate to the possibilities offered by trade for importing a broader array of less expensive or higher-quality products than is available on the domestic market and for exposing domestic suppliers to greater competition in an orderly, adjustment-promoting manner, as well as for attracting foreign investment in key sectors.

Service negotiations represent a unique opportunity for countries at all levels of development to secure more favorable terms of access to foreign service markets that reliance on unilateral reform alone is not able to provide. The preparations needed to put together informed requests can also benefit from the regulatory inventories and capacity-building efforts described above. But additional matters must be addressed if a country is to assemble development-enhancing requests.

Request lists are offensive (as opposed to defensive). They focus on sectors, subsectors, and modes of supply relative to which the requesting countries are asking partner countries progressively to remove or lessen access-impairing regulatory measures. The main motivation behind request lists is the promotion of the export interests of the leading service providers of the requesting country. The content of a country's request list should therefore be based on an assessment of these interests, which is absent in the approach many developing countries take to the negotiations.

In theory, nothing prevents a country from asking for commitments in all sectors included under service agreements. The reason such an outcome normally does not arise in practice is that countries are often reluctant to formulate requests in areas where they may not be in a position to offer reciprocal concessions. This may explain why relatively few developing countries took part in the collective requests formulated after the WTO Ministerial Conference held in Hong Kong, China, in December 2005.

Putting together targeted negotiating requests requires detailed information about the measures that are hindering access to the markets of key trading partners. The breadth of the service trade and the diversity of the sectors involved render information-gathering a large and complex task with which many developing countries, even larger ones, experience recurring difficulties. The difficulties are compounded if the channels of communication with key stakeholders (that is, chambers of commerce, service firms already active in world markets, firms in active prospecting mode, embassies in key foreign markets, and so on) are inadequate. This highlights the potential payoff of targeted trade-related technical assistance aimed at providing developing-country suppliers with economic intelligence on the conditions and opportunities for access to, for example, export markets, distribution channels, information on product standards, and business-to-business dialoguing and networking.

The ultimate strategy in service negotiations and the position papers, offers, requests, and other relevant documents needed to implement the strategy must also reflect awareness of matters unrelated to services. Trade negotiations are typically organized as a single undertaking, whereby nothing is agreed until everything has been agreed. Thus, service negotiations are often, if not always, part of a larger context that includes all sectors of an economy.[8] As the Doha negotiations have made clear, negotiations on agriculture and industrial products exert a huge impact on the nature and pace of the negotiations on services, including what is being demanded, what is being offered, the overall approach to the negotiations, and even the outstanding rules and principles that may also be under negotiation. In addition to the concerns relating to the service sector, a negotiating strategy for services must therefore reflect an awareness of the limits and opportunities emerging from other elements of the single undertaking under negotiation. This draws attention to the need for policy coordination among the ministries and members of a country's trade negotiating team.

The range of pertinent concerns that arises in carrying out service negotiations is outlined in box 2.7.

Implementing Negotiated Outcomes

The agreements emerging from the Uruguay Round established a broad set of obligations for developing economies that went well beyond the traditional border measures of the General Agreement on Tariffs and Trade and included disciplines with a far wider development impact. This is clear in services, with their coverage of sectors such as finance, telecommunications, and transportation that possess critical economy-wide, infrastructural properties, as well as sectors in which a host of public policy concerns and sensitivities arise, such as health care, education, environmental, and audiovisual services.

While trade-related capacity building has contributed to the ability of developing economies to formulate and negotiate national strategies in trade, this does not necessarily mean that they are able to implement trade agreements, nor does it guarantee the availability of the resources required to cover the significant recurring costs that new trade rules in

Box 2.7

Concerns Arising in Service Negotiations

- Has the government identified the specific rule-making issues to which it intends to attach priority in service negotiations?
- How adequate are the negotiating skills of the country's trade and regulatory officials, particularly their capacity to take an active part in discussions on rule-making issues in service negotiations?
- Has the government considered teaming up with other WTO members or regional partners to formulate proposals and negotiate on selected rule-making issues?
- Has the government considered how to cooperate with various international organizations, bilateral donors, or expert nongovernmental organizations in formulating negotiating proposals on rule-making, market-opening, or development issues?
- Has the government considered the pros and cons of participating in collective requests and offers on rule-making, thematic, or sectoral issues so as to overcome resource constraints and achieve scale economies in negotiations?
- What role is the government assigning to article XVIII (additional commitments) of the GATS (and PTA equivalents) in sequencing liberalization undertakings (precommitting to opening) or in addressing sector-specific complements of market opening (government procurement, emergency safeguards, issues related to labor mobility, and so on)?
- What criteria does the government apply to choose among measures, modes of supply, and the sectors that are to be offered as bound, partially bound, or unbound in negotiations?
- Has a clear distinction been established between the defensive and offensive interests in the negotiations?
- Are the country's negotiating red lines clearly established, and does a process exist to revisit these in light of developments within and outside service negotiations?
- Have export interests been identified so as to contribute to the elaboration of a realistic request list?
- How does the government compile information on the foreign barriers affecting the country's service suppliers?
- Has a mock request list been drawn up on the basis of existing information?

(continued)

Box 2.7 *(continued)*

- What procedure does the ministry responsible for service negotiations use to seek input from key stakeholders in responding to the requests for market opening formulated by trading partners?
- Do consultations focus primarily on targeted sectors and key domestic suppliers, or is an attempt made to weigh the economy-wide implications of acceding to negotiating requests?
- Does the government weigh the pros and cons of binding less than the status quo, notably, in terms of the signals such a decision may send regarding the country's investment and regulatory climate?
- To what extent is the government's negotiating stance in services, notably, as regards the evolution of liberalization offers, informed by and coordinated with the state of play of negotiations in nonservice sectors?

highly regulated sectors typically generate. These costs may be associated with a range of initiatives, from strengthening regulatory agencies to the establishment of independent regulatory agencies in telecommunications or energy.

The administrative and financial burdens of complying with WTO obligations tend to be particularly acute in WTO-acceding economies, especially the least developed economies, because accession is almost certain to involve far-reaching commitments to substantive legal and institutional reforms. Moreover, the costs linked with the implementation of WTO agreements or PTAs do not revolve solely around legal compliance. The costs also encompass the ancillary measures and costs that must be covered to obtain and support *effectively* the benefits deriving from implementation and liberalization. These costs and capacity-building requirements vary according to domestic circumstances; in resource-constrained environments, they may, at times, need to be assessed against competing and more compelling domestic priorities.

Addressing Regulatory Weaknesses
One area in which trade-related technical assistance can make a decisive contribution in services is in strengthening regulatory agencies in developing countries. Regulatory institutions are costly and require staff with sophisticated legal and economic skills. As the current financial crisis in

developed-country markets reminds us, sound domestic regulation is critical to realizing the benefits of open service markets and in responding to potential downsides.

To engage meaningfully in service negotiations, a government must be confident in its ability to manage the regulatory, sectoral, and economy-wide implications of liberalization. In assessing its capacities in the production and exchange of services, it must confront any competitive weaknesses that result from its regulatory regime. Onerous regulatory requirements may prevent a country's enterprises in a particular sector from increasing the economic efficiency of their operations or from introducing new, more competitive services and marketing techniques.

Many service sectors are highly regulated as a consequence of policy objectives. Examples are consumer protection, equitable or universal access to services in health care and education, environmental protection, and, in the case of financial services, the protection of depositors and the maintenance of financial stability. This regulation forms an essential part of good governance and a functioning market economy. Accordingly, both the GATS and preferential service agreements recognize the right of countries to regulate and introduce new regulations on the supply of services so as to meet national policy objectives.

Trade liberalization in services may intersect with domestic regulation in two main ways. First, in making regulations, governments must take into account many factors, one of which may be the economy-wide trade and investment impacts of the regulation. Information on the potential economic, trade, and investment costs may assist governments in finding most efficient regulatory tools for achieving desired policy objectives. There are likely to be positive effects in terms of democratic governance from the more efficient and transparent design, implementation, and enforcement of domestic regulations.

Second, the process of liberalizing service markets may require new or different types of regulatory interventions, for example, to ensure that the expected benefits of liberalization are realized (for instance, that liberalization results in a genuinely competitive market) or that important policy objectives are achieved within the new market structures (for instance, universal service obligations).

Procompetitive regulatory reform need not be an exercise in regulatory disarmament. It is precisely because service sector liberalization often requires significant new regulation that governments, particularly those with weak regulatory capacities, may be loath to undertake far-reaching liberalization commitments in the context of trade agreements.

Nonetheless, as the discussion on the desirability of performing a trade-related regulatory audit suggests (see box 2.3), the process and culture of the regulatory reform and review that trade negotiations may help to promote involve key issues, including, but not limited to, the following:

- *The purpose or policy objective of the regulation:* for example, consumer or environmental protection, prudential protection, ensuring competition or equitable and universal access to a service, reducing income and regional disparities
- *The effectiveness and efficiency of the regulation:* factors to consider may include the reasonableness, objectivity, and transparency of the regulation; whether the regulation is proportional to the objective being pursued; whether the regulation is linked to or rooted in international standards
- *Implementation of the regulation:* for example, are there transparent and impartial procedures for implementing the regulation? Can natural and juridical persons affected by the regulation provide input prior to the adoption of the regulation? Do natural and juridical persons negatively affected by the regulation have any recourse through appeal? Do the relevant ministries or government agencies have the skills, financial resources, and political legitimacy to carry out their regulatory and implementation responsibilities?

These points are merely indicative. Countries may not consider the points important, or they may assign importance to other factors. Weighing the value of each factor, while essential for effective liberalization that serves national objectives, including development or equity objectives, can be a challenging process, particularly in developing countries with limited administrative capacity. Many countries require significant technical assistance in regulatory capacity building and in training and assistance in the implementation of commitments after market opening.

In engaging in service negotiations, governments must have some idea of the desirable duration of the transition toward greater market openness. Liberalization cannot be achieved overnight, particularly in service markets; it is typically best pursued in a progressive, orderly, and transparent manner. This allows incumbents to prepare for greater competition, anticipate the possible distributional downside, and put in place a proper regulatory framework.

The complexity and slow pace of domestic regulatory reform in many service markets imply that countries prefer a sequenced approach to market opening. Proper sequencing can help overcome the concerns of providers of domestic services about the greater competitive challenges. Recourse to progressive liberalization may also buy time for regulatory authorities to acquire the expertise to regulate more open domestic markets and to anticipate and manage the new market risks that the openness may entail.

There is little doubt that adopting and implementing sounder regulations are key to a better overall performance in services. Often, regulations trigger positive externalities through facilitated trade and investment, an improved investment climate, and procompetitive regulatory stances. This is why, in services, efforts directed at assisting developing countries to adopt best practice regulatory regimes and to benchmark the regulatory regimes according to international standards may be of considerable benefit.

It appears desirable, if one considers how to serve the service-related aid for trade needs of developing countries, to distinguish countries by income level. This typically represents a sound proxy for regulatory sophistication and absorptive capacity in services. Least developed countries are likely to be better served by regional and multilateral development agencies with a greater local presence, tighter ongoing monitoring, and a finer appreciation of the country- or region-specific institutional and human resource constraints. Nonetheless, countries with more advanced regulatory and implementation capacities are likely to have a keener interest in best practice regulation and in learning from other emerging countries and developed-country counterparts in areas of mutual regulatory interest.

Greater efforts must be directed at providing opportunities for developing-country officials to train in programs on trade and sectoral regulation in leading institutions of higher education and in relevant international organizations with sectoral expertise.[9]

Other options include capacity-building activities that embed donor country expertise within regulatory agencies in recipient countries, as well as the pairing of local institutions and leading universities or policy research institutions. Examples of such training and regulatory strengthening are the European Union–China Trade Project and the International Trade Assistance Project in Indonesia, which is funded by the U.S. Agency for International Development (box 2.8). Trade and investment liberalization is hardly without distributional consequences. The gains and losses arising from a change in the domestic conditions of competition affect groups in society, and a careful assessment must take account of the

Box 2.8

Examples of Best Practice Capacity Building in Services

The European Union–China Trade Project. Between March 2005 and December 2008, China and the European Union carried out a range of bilateral activities in the trade in services, including the following:

- In China, 14 conferences and seminars were held on topics such as financial services; state treasury management; the environment, climate change, and financial services; professional licensing in legal services; the development of the information technology and communication industry; measures to develop China's insurance and financial markets; civil aviation; and competition policy challenges in service industries.
- Also in China, 12 studies were carried out on subjects such as domestic regulation, outsourcing financial services, insurance market openness, insurance supervision, policies in mergers and acquisitions in banking services, urban planning and commercial centers, air transportation and the GATS, deregulation of the aviation sector, the effects of liberalization in retail distribution services, and the travel industry.
- Seven tours by Chinese delegations in the European Union examined the regulation of foreign legal consultants, bankruptcy regulations for financial institutions, payment and settlement systems, the regulation of legal services, and service statistics.
- Chinese internship programs were hosted in various European institutions concerned with trade, economics, and regulatory matters.

Several best practice lessons in services emerge from the design of the European Union–China Trade Project. The project is focusing policy research attention on the second generation of implementation challenges arising following WTO accession. For the most part, this entails working in close proximity with key regulatory agencies, ministries, and China's Ministry of Commerce in ensuring that the implementing legislation in China is consistent with WTO provisions and the country's accession commitments. The presence of a team of experts (around 15 professionals), both Chinese and European, in Beijing greatly facilitates this task and is creating sectoral knowledge and indigenous capacity in project management, while favoring greater responsiveness to client needs. The project has hired the former deputy head of the mission of China to the WTO during the closing phase of the accession negotiations. A person of such high rank is valuable in

(continued)

Box 2.8 *(continued)*

working closely with the Chinese bureaucracy. The project team is in regular consultation with the representatives in Beijing of the European Commission and typically involves commission staff, whether residing in Beijing or traveling from Brussels, in project seminars, conferences, and other activities in China. The interaction has also facilitated the exchange of policy messages between the two partners.

Foreign and local experts drawn from leading Chinese universities and research institutions have been associated in project technical studies on regulatory and sectoral issues. A similar approach has been used in organizing seminars at which the findings of research are discussed among experts from China and abroad.

Another best practice component of the European Union–China Trade Project is the project's emphasis on training. Each year for the past three years, the project has funded the participation of two or three Ministry of Commerce staff to follow the year-long Masters of International Law and Economics Program at the World Trade Institute in Bern, one of the world's leading centers of policy research and advanced training in trade regulation. Moreover, mindful of the need to secure regulatory compliance among Chinese subnational (provincial) governments, the project has also funded the participation of local officials in a five-week summer academy held each year at the World Trade Institute. In 2007–08, more than 30 officials in provincial governments benefited from advanced training during the summer academy.

The Indonesia Trade Assistance Project. The US$13.5 million, four-year Indonesia Trade Assistance Project was funded and implemented by the U.S. Agency for International Development in 2004–08. The project delivery was outsourced to Chemonics International, leading U.S. development consultants with wide experience in trade-related technical assistance and capacity building.

The project focused training efforts on legal support, economic research, public outreach, organizational development, and information technology. Delivered by a team of U.S. and local experts working at the Indonesian Department of Trade, it aimed to improve the capacity of the department to analyze and implement trade reforms that would lead to increased exports, a more attractive investment climate, and expanded employment opportunities for Indonesians.

The project funded and oversaw the development of a one-year Master's Program in Trade Policy and Negotiations at the country's leading university,

(continued)

Box 2.8 *(continued)*

Universitas Indonesia. The program is directed partly toward Department of Trade staff. A full-term (15-week) course on trade in services was developed to this end.

A measure of the effectiveness of a locally anchored capacity-building project of this type is the activities the project supported. These included capacity strengthening among Department of Trade staff; a workshop series on economic research and trade policy analysis; a trade research lecture series; mentoring in economic research and trade policy analysis; briefing sessions for Department of Trade staff by project economists; the strengthening of the links between the Department of Trade and Indonesia's leading universities and research institutions working on trade issues; funding, development, and delivery by project staff and local academics of a one-year Master's Program in Economics in International Trade Policy, in association with the law and economics faculties at Universitas Indonesia; specialized training for Department of Trade lawyers and the legal staff in relevant departments and regulatory agencies; the launch, in 2009, of a new Master's Program on International Trade Law at Universitas Indonesia; outreach activities with law schools in the greater Jakarta area; publication of a textbook on WTO law in Indonesian; upgrades in the information technology facilities and staff of the Department of Trade; and the promotion of a public-private dialogue on the WTO and Indonesia's regional trade policy.

Sources: Cardno 2009; Chemonics International 2008.

impact of liberalization on vulnerable groups (including the workers in state-owned enterprises likely to face greater postliberalization dislocation), as well as the interests of poor, small, and geographically remote firms, all of which may experience more limited access to finance.

Another candidate for enhanced assistance in the implementation phase is thus the design of reforms that factor in the distributional impacts of liberalization on population segments (rural versus urban, formal versus informal, men versus women and children) and improve the access of these people to essential services. These services range from sanitation to transportation, telecommunications, small-scale finance, education, and health care. While most of the policy challenges lie outside the realm of trade negotiations, finding the correct solutions can help build support for the opening of markets. However, implementing these policies in an economically sound manner may present numerous problems for weak bureaucracies, and many developing countries require support and time in addressing the difficulties.

Much of the delivery of trade-related technical assistance, including in the service trade, involves short training activities. Effective course design, delivery, and, above all, attention to the context are critical ingredients. Box 2.9 highlights several best practices in trade-related technical assistance design and delivery drawn from Australia's recent experience in Indonesia.

Box 2.9

Best Practices in Trade-Related Training: Course Design and Delivery

Best practices may be employed in delivering technical training to government officials through the typical short-term course formats within which the bulk of trade-related technical assistance in services is delivered. The purpose of the training is to ensure that the skills and capabilities of staff in the trade ministries, line ministries, or regulatory agencies concerned with trade negotiations and implementation matters are durably upgraded. The two main areas on which effective training resides are course design and course delivery. Courses that are effectively designed have the following main characteristics:

- They are tied to the ministry's strategic vision, mission statements, and main functions.
- They are conducted in a location free of office distractions. Training courses of less than a week may take place in the capital, but all training should occur outside the office. Longer-term training should be located far enough away to prevent staff from being called back to their offices.
- They provide participants with training materials that are specifically tailored to the country's problems and the ministry's needs.
- They are carried out in coordination with other providers of training to the ministry to avoid overlaps or substantive inconsistencies.
- They target the most suitable participants, that is, those for whom the training is directly relevant.

While most training tends to be aimed at junior or new professional staff, the training needs of more senior managers often require attention because of the expertise of the latter, the greater pressures they face (especially if trade expertise is

(continued)

Box 2.9 *(continued)*

scarce and concentrated among a few managers), and the reluctance of senior managers to engage in training activities. Training courses among senior staff should be short, involve fewer people, and allow close interaction with the invited experts. Training that is effectively delivered has the following main characteristics:

- It requires participants to produce outputs relevant to supporting the ministry in achieving its mission statement and strategic vision. An example would be a paper or briefing note for the minister.
- It provides an interactive format to offer more opportunities for transferring knowledge; examples would be case studies, practical exercises, and group sessions. It requires participants to be active because this is the best way to ensure the transfer of knowledge.
- It is delivered as a series of courses that incrementally build up the skills and capabilities of participants. This allows participants to apply their newly acquired knowledge in the office after each training session.
- It is pitched at a level that is appropriate for the participants.
- It is delivered in the local language, or, if the training is delivered in a foreign language by international experts, all training materials should be translated into the local language.

Source: AusAID 2007.

Box 2.10 contains questions that emerge about the implementation phase of the trade negotiation cycle in services.

Enhancing the Capacity to Supply

The last pillar of a coherent negotiating package in services should target the constraints that many developing-country exporters face in supplying newly opened markets. Despite the success stories in sectors such as energy, business-process outsourcing, construction, and environmental services, there are too few documented examples of developing-country companies significantly involved in the export trade.

There are several explanations for this. Thus, most service firms are small, including firms in the countries of the Organisation for Economic Co-operation and Development. Small service suppliers typically have limited human resources to build referral networks, find partners abroad, identify market opportunities, and research the regulatory conditions in

Box 2.10

The Implementation Phase of the Service Trade Negotiation Cycle

- Do proposed new or improved commitments reflect an assessment of the implementation costs (including recurring costs) related to regulatory enforcement activities?
- Has a proper assessment been made of the capacity-strengthening needs of regulatory agencies prior to scheduling new or improved commitments?
- Has the government given thought to formulating requests for capacity-strengthening as a precondition or quid pro quo for new or improved commitments?
- What considerations weigh on the government's decision to pursue liberalization in a progressive manner and sequence liberalization with strengthened regulatory and implementation capacities?
- Is the government considering making use of article XVIII (additional commitments) of the GATS (and its PTA equivalents) in adopting a sequenced approach linking market opening with the strengthening of regulatory and implementation capacities?
- Has an attempt been made to benchmark the country's regulatory practices and institutions according to those of key trading partners or of countries at similar levels of development and regulatory sophistication?
- To what extent might regulatory harmonization or the pursuit of mutual recognition initiatives help countries address weaknesses in domestic regulatory practices, help overcome the trade-inhibiting effects of regulatory diversity, and move domestic regulatory regimes toward best regional or global practices?
- To what extent does the government's liberalization strategy and its approach to sequencing reflect an ex ante assessment of the possible social, environmental, and developmental impacts of market opening?
- Is the government confident in its analytical capacity to conduct the various impact assessments linked to service sector liberalization, or does it require dedicated technical assistance?
- Have attempts been made to learn, through targeted training, from the postliberalization implementation experience of neighboring countries or countries at similar levels of development?

foreign markets. In many market segments, such as telecommunications, utilities, finance, and transportation, developing-country firms must also contend with the large fixed costs of entering capital-intensive sectors, as well as with the presence of large companies in the market. Even in sectors in which developing countries are exporting, studies reveal that their exporters are facing key common problems, including (1) market development constraints flowing from low brand recognition and difficulties in establishing credibility with international suppliers;[10] (2) lack of access to financing for export or business development;[11] (3) limited prospects to serve foreign markets through an established presence (that is, more limited returns on Mode 3 commitments by trading partners); (4) lack of access to reliable and inexpensive infrastructure and key input services, notably, finance, information technology, and telecommunications; and (5) lack of access to the range of formal and informal networks and institutional facilities necessary for trade (see OECD 2003, Chaitoo 2008).

Typically, developing economies must diversify and add value to their production chains and export baskets. This requires, first and foremost, enhanced access to foreign markets and a progressive lifting of the impediments to trade, investment, and labor movement facing service suppliers, which is the essence of what trade negotiations can deliver. Yet, securing durable gains in supply capacity requires efforts on several other fronts as well. Chief among these are efforts to raise quality standards, meet host-country certification requirements, and improve home-country trade infrastructure, notably, through higher quality and lower cost in communications, finance, transportation, and logistics services.

Governments, the private sector, and development partners must invent new ways to work together to foster competitive supply responses. This is arguably the most difficult element in the service negotiating cycle because matters relating to private sector development tend to involve expertise and institutions that are not centrally involved in previous parts of the negotiating life cycle. Still, experience shows that important trade performance payoffs may result from targeting development assistance toward intermediary (or meso-level) institutions and processes, such as private sector associations, support structures for small and medium enterprises, and public-private dialogue and partnering activities.

Until now, the aid-for-trade debate has largely centered on support for the public sector rather than the private sector (see elsewhere below). Aid for trade financing has also shown a distinct bias toward nonservice activities.[12] While one should not discount the difficulties that public sector entities face in preparing for and conducting trade negotiations and implementing the outcomes, commercial capacity constraints also exist in the private sector. These constraints may hamper the ability of countries and firms to take advantage of new trade and investment opportunities.

The reason for the focus of assistance primarily on public sector entities can be traced to the nature and mandates of the regional and multilateral suppliers of trade-related technical assistance, which represent mainly the interests of national governments or regional regulatory or negotiating entities. However, this bias also has its origin in the dearth of instruments of knowledge and policy aimed specifically at helping developing-country firms expand the service trade. Redressing the bias in the design and delivery of service- and trade-related technical assistance is critical to lifting the constraints on service exporting firms in developing countries.

While the governments of countries at all levels of development face numerous challenges in understanding how to maximize the economic benefits and the benefits for service suppliers from a fuller engagement in service trade negotiations, the challenges are clearly more acute for developing countries.

There are several reasons for this. First, governments often have incomplete information about the current status of service trade activities within their borders. Most export development initiatives focus on the trade in goods, and service exporters have therefore become used to operating independently of government programs. For this reason, government officials typically possess only anecdotal evidence on service export activities. This problem is reinforced by the shortage in service trade statistics that arises, in part, because there is not a convenient checkpoint, such as a border crossing, at which trade data may be collected on services. Most WTO members lack not only information about the services being exported and about export markets, but also registries of service exporters to whom they might address queries.

Second, most governments do not collect detailed statistics on the services that firms or households purchase and, so, do not have usefully disaggregated data on service inputs into sectors of the economy. This hinders efforts to measure the impact on the domestic economy of liberalizing or restricting the access to foreign providers of services.

Third, in most countries, including developed economies, up to 95 percent of service firms are small and, so, are often underrepresented in statistical surveys because of the response burdens such surveys represent. In addition, small firms typically do not have staff dedicated to government relations and therefore do not participate actively in government trade consultations.

Fourth, service trade agreements are relatively new and have tended to offer relatively few liberalization benefits, other than transparency, in key foreign markets. Thus, service exporters and importers have not been highly motivated to participate in government consultations.

Finally, advocacy groups such as industry associations are still largely unaware of the service export activities of their smaller members and are therefore not always able to represent the interests of these members. In many countries, industry associations in services are relatively less developed than their counterparts in manufacturing and agriculture.

To negotiate effectively, identify the interests, competitive strengths, and weaknesses of domestic suppliers more accurately, and direct policy attention to the need for more supply capacity, governments, in consultation with domestic stakeholders, should consider a range of objectives (box 2.11).

Box 2.11

The Strengths and Weaknesses of Domestic Suppliers

Learn about the exporters, the services exported, the export markets, and the supply modes. A major purpose of negotiations is to strengthen the competitive positioning of a country's service exporters. If a government is unaware of the competitive strengths of the economy, it may inadvertently ignore or undermine domestic service exporters at the negotiating table. Especially developing economies often assume there is little export activity in service markets. Yet, research by the International Trade Centre has indicated that many developing-country firms export more than 40 different types of services to many export markets. Developing countries may thus have greater export interests and potential in the trade in services than the governments conducting the negotiations recognize.

Learn about the essentials of the competitiveness of service firms. To develop negotiating positions, governments must understand the nontariff or regulatory obstacles that local service exporters are encountering according to the mode of supply and within the sectors of the exporters or across related sectors. For the request process, governments must also determine priority export markets. This is challenging because the global competitive environment in services is rapidly

(continued)

Box 2.11 *(continued)*

changing, and service exporters operate across a range of markets that is wider than the range of markets for goods exporters. Because firms may more easily enter new service markets if the firms have advocates who appreciate the quality of the services being provided, important export markets for the firms are likely to include the home markets of foreign investors in the firms, markets with significant expatriate populations, markets in countries that are regular travel destinations of consumers of the products of the firms, and markets in countries with which the home countries of the firms have reached economic integration agreements.

Determine the role of service imports and ensure the economic benefits of liberal market access. The competitiveness of all domestic enterprises, as well as the quality of the lives of citizens, depends on the type and quality of the available service inputs. The existence of the option to import can provide a competitive incentive to improve the quality and availability of imports. Foreign firms that choose to establish local offices may also create jobs and generate other positive spillovers, especially in terms of improved product standards, better access to distributional channels, and so on.

Build domestic support for service trade liberalization by identifying national champions. Perhaps because service agreements are complex and deal with many issues that affect the quality of people's lives, they often become the focal point of broader concerns about globalization. Civil society actors have expressed the fear that service trade rules may infringe on domestic regulatory sovereignty, disrupt basic services (such as education, health care, and utilities), favor foreign over domestic interests, and limit environmental obligations. These and similar fears often overlook the degree of choice involved in making sectoral commitments under trade agreements such as the GATS and the role of service firms in creating the vast majority of new jobs. It is important to foster an informed public debate about service liberalization, including by creating opportunities for a dialogue between service exporters (especially small firms) and representatives of relevant public interest groups. Identifying and partnering with firms, including small firms, that have become successful exporters of services can he helpful in addressing the legitimate public policy concerns that negotiations in areas characterized by high regulatory intensity and particular policy sensitivities may generate.

Source: OECD 2002.

It is particularly important that the private sector acquire a voice in the trade negotiation process and speak to the needs of service users and providers. Assisting in the creation, early funding, and nurturing of sustainable coalitions of service industries in developing countries represents a new type of trade-related technical assistance in the service trade. It involves direct business-to-business dialogue supported by donor governments (box 2.12).

Box 2.12

Organizing Service Coalitions in Developing Countries

The integration of services in the multilateral trading system during the Uruguay Round and the subsequent liberalization processes that followed at the bilateral, regional, and multilateral levels alerted major private sector stakeholders, particularly in developed countries, to the necessity of monitoring these processes and influencing rules and negotiated outcomes to their advantage.

A need has arisen in a number of countries to establish organized service-related private sector advocacy groups mandated by industry associations and enterprises to lobby relevant governmental and nongovernmental constituencies and give voice to corporate interests in and concerns about issues in the service trade.

The private sector in some developed countries has taken the lead in creating coalitions of service industries that serve as umbrella organizations, establishing informal networks that share a common interest in the development of service industries, and bringing together service firms and business associations to discuss policy issues and identify strategies.

Although some of the coalitions in developed countries were organized prior to or during the course of the Uruguay Round, the majority were created after the conclusion of the round. Most of these coalitions operate through small, flexible secretariats. They tend to represent the interests of larger service enterprises, which may not always correspond to the interests of small and medium enterprises. However, the interests of small and medium enterprises can readily be taken into consideration through the affiliation of these enterprises with sectoral service associations that are members of larger coalitions. The majority of the coalitions represent private sector companies, and governments have no institutional role. This enables the coalitions to discuss and coordinate freely, independently formulate policies, and undertake activities in a manner that reflects only their interests.

(continued)

Box 2.12 *(continued)*

Coalitions are more common in high-income countries. This may be attributed to a host of factors, including the lack of awareness in many developing countries of the important role of services in their economies, the lack of adequate funding, and the prevalence of forces that are not supportive of public-private collaboration and that are unwilling to endorse the concept of institutionalizing private sector policy advocacy mechanisms.

Few existing coalitions are dedicated solely to advancing their interests in regional and multilateral trade negotiations. In almost all cases, mandates encompass objectives of a more domestic nature such as establishing internal databases on export opportunities in foreign markets, achieving improvements in service sector statistics and data, enhancing public and private awareness on the strategic economic and social role of services, and encouraging governments to implement domestic economic, fiscal, and monetary policies that promote a service-friendly environment.

Policy advocacy by service coalitions: The impact on trade policies. Service sector coalitions in developed countries tend to have significantly wider mandates and, consequently, more extensive constituencies and larger spheres of interest than their developing-country counterparts. While the lobbying of the latter has been limited to government constituencies, the concerns of the former typically encompass legislative constituencies, government constituencies in foreign markets, and other stakeholders. Some member companies in developed-country coalitions enjoy considerable political weight in their own right because of their size and global reach.

Given their greater financial and human resource capacity and sophistication, developed-country coalitions are generally more active and aggressive in lobbying national constituencies, which, in many instances, is sustained by institutionalized consultation processes. Some developed-country coalitions understand that, if they are to achieve their export goals in foreign markets, their own governments must also address the export interests of trading partners.

This is readily apparent in the case of the Coalition of Service Industries, which has, for years, lobbied the U.S. Trade Representative and the U.S. Congress to ease the restrictions on the service and nonservice exports of trading partners through WTO negotiations. In return, U.S. trading partners may, it is hoped, become more engaged in opening their service markets in sectors of interest to the exporters among the coalition members.

(continued)

Box 2.12 *(continued)*

Besides private sector service industry coalitions, other national, regional, and international advocates also play an important role in voicing the interests of the industry in multilateral and preferential trade negotiations, although their inputs generally address services more comprehensively by also covering negotiations on the trade in agricultural and nonagricultural goods and other areas. Among the most active lobbying advocates at the international level is the International Chamber of Commerce.

It is difficult to document the influence of service industry coalitions on service trade liberalization. There is, however, significant anecdotal evidence suggesting that such coalitions are among the most effective in influencing government positions in service trade negotiations. The advocacy activities of coalitions may be more significant in bilateral and regional trade negotiations, in which, unlike the multilateral trade process, member states may have greater leverage, address policy concerns over shorter time frames, and pursue more narrowly defined trade, investment, and regulatory objectives with partner countries.

Future challenges and opportunities. Service sector coalitions face several key challenges, as follows: (1) the heterogeneous nature of the service sector and the conflicting intersectoral interests that occasionally arise from this diversity, which heightens the challenge of achieving coordination; (2) the antiglobalization backlash that often targets the alleged dangers service sector liberalization represents for the domestic policy space, social security, employment, or access to public services; (3) the adverse implications of the lobbying by influential nonservice private sector players, which have sometimes succeeded in focusing government attention on other economic sectors, notably, agriculture, regardless of the importance of these sectors (relative to the importance of services) to economies; and (4) the burden to draw attention to the significance of the service sector in the formulation of trade policies. This last challenge tends to be augmented because of budgetary constraints.

However, despite the challenges and the existence of few effective coalitions in developing countries, the number and organizational quality of service industry coalitions will increase because of the following factors: (1) the rapidly growing economic importance of services in the developed countries and the developing countries and the increasing appreciation of the vital role of services in shaping economic policy making and trends in international trade; (2) the mounting desire of national and multinational service companies to organize

(continued)

Box 2.12 *(continued)*

together to enhance their ability to explore new export markets and develop advocacy initiatives able to influence national, regional, and multilateral trade policies; (3) the integration of more service-related trade and investment rules and liberalization commitments in bilateral, regional, and multilateral trade agreements; and (4) the expanding role played by coalitions, mainly in developed countries, in assisting in the establishment of similar coalitions in the developing world by sharing organizational and policy advocacy experience. International organizations can play a vital capacity-building role. This is the case of the International Trade Centre, which, through its World Trade Net Program, is providing support so that service industry communities in developing countries become organized and are able to defend their interests and reach their objectives.

Source: El-Etreby 2008.

Because of its focus on the private sector, capacity building to address supply-side constraints involves institutional actors that are different from the actors concerned with strengthening trade negotiating or regulatory capacity. The difference is important in the design of assistance and in interagency coordination. This is an area in which greater involvement by private sector service exporters in industrialized countries might usefully complement the efforts of bilateral donors and multilateral agencies such as the International Trade Centre or the World Bank.

Service exporters in industrialized countries also have a stake in ensuring that developing-country markets become open in a sustainable manner and within a stable regulatory environment. This objective can be served through enhanced private sector support for regulatory institutions and best practices in developing countries. The private sector must contribute financial resources, staff, and expertise to efforts to enhance regulatory performance, improve quality and licensing standards and compliance with these standards, and expand the access to distribution networks.

Substantial payoffs may also flow from targeted trade-related technical assistance to provide developing-country suppliers with better economic intelligence on access conditions and opportunities in export markets and distribution channels, information on product standards, business-to-business dialogue and networking, and so on.

The lack of straightforward information on domestic regulatory procedures, including licensing and product certification, and the lack of market intelligence rank among the biggest commercial barriers to the service exports of developing countries. Mechanisms must be implemented in developed countries and leading emerging economies that replace passive enquiry and contact points by helping predominantly small servicers contest markets in advanced countries. The countries of the Organisation for Economic Co-operation and Development and leading emerging economies need to give meaning to the commitments they made under GATS article IV (the increasing participation of developing countries) and the PTA equivalents by offering tangible support for market access by developing-country suppliers. Meeting these and other challenges can be facilitated through the work of dedicated agencies such as the Centre for the Promotion of Imports in the Netherlands and the Trade Facilitation Office Canada (box 2.13).

Box 2.13

Providing Market Intelligence to Developing-Country Suppliers: The Trade Facilitation Office, Canada

Established by the Canadian International Development Agency in 1980, the Trade Facilitation Office Canada is a nonprofit corporation. Its mandate is to assist exporters in developing countries and transition economies in securing greater access to the Canadian market. It does this by offering these exporters practical advice, market information, and exposure in the Canadian marketplace through various promotional activities.

The main services of the office include the following: (1) Canadian market information services is a Web-based source of information on export requirements and market intelligence targeted at small and medium enterprises in developing countries. For a fee, the office also provides exporters with tailored market development consulting services, information seminars, trade missions, and so on. The office also publishes an electronic newsletter containing sourcing information for would-be exporters to Canada. (2) Trade-readiness capacity building services focus on training and the implementation of trade development projects with local partners so as to enhance the skills of developing-country exporters and strengthen institutions in developing countries to attract trade and investment.

(continued)

Box 2.13 *(continued)*

While the experience of the office in services is limited, it has begun to devote more attention to the sector to develop service offerings suited to the sector and aimed at helping developing-country exporters, particularly small and medium enterprises, understand the fragmented Canadian market for services, gain a surer foothold in this market, and reach out to Canadian consumers (through Mode 2 trade, for example, consumption abroad) in areas such as health-related tourism and wellness. The office has also produced a market report on the Canadian service sector, focusing particularly on tourism and selected business services (TFO Canada 2008). The report is intended to provide developing-country suppliers with background information on the service sector in Canada to facilitate (1) the development of a strategy for entering the Canadian market, (2) an understanding of the complex nature of the service industry in Canada, (3) an appreciation of the costs involved in entering this market, and (4) the acquisition of additional information from other sources before entering the market.

The office occupies a unique niche in private sector development. Canadian negotiators have recently begun to make its services known to trading partners, particularly PTA partners, to signal the attention Canada pays to service issues and other sectors of priority interest to developing countries.

Source: Trade Facilitation Office Canada, http://www.tfocanada.ca.

Coalitions of service industries in emerging economies and in various countries in the Organisation for Economic Co-operation and Development can play a role in establishing business-to-business contacts, especially among small and medium enterprises. Funding assistance by governments for private sector development might also prove helpful.

The multiplicity of modes of service supply and the related regulatory intensity in the service trade and in factor movements raise additional challenges in the provision of technical assistance to buttress supply capacities. The dominance of commercial presence as a service supply mode suggests that assistance directed at enhancing the investment climate in a host country may be important in strengthening service sector competitiveness and eliciting an adequate private sector response through foreign direct investment. Beyond providing scarce capital, inflows of foreign direct investment in goods and services can be expected to create opportunities for local suppliers in many service sectors (for example, telecommunications, transportation, logistics, finance, and professional and business services) and enhance access to the distribution channels of multinational enterprises in other markets. Particular attention should be devoted to assistance targeted at the creation of a toolkit for the promotion of foreign direct investment and offering advice on best practices in the design and implementation of investment incentive schemes in various service industries.

Meanwhile, the rising importance of crossborder trade and the remote supply of service markets highlights the need for greater regulatory convergence through the adoption of international standards and the negotiation of mutual recognition agreements to facilitate greater crossborder service trade. Poor standards and inadequacies in domestic regulation frustrate the access of developing-country services and service providers to foreign markets. Helping developing countries improve the quality and standards of domestic services, notably, by strengthening participation in regional or global standard-setting initiatives is another area in which capacity building may be expected to yield development dividends. Questions that may arise in the provision of assistance to strengthen the supply-side capacity of developing-country service exporters are shown in box 2.14.

Box 2.14

Strengthening the Supply-Side Capacity of Developing-Country Exporters

- Which advisory services and training opportunities have been developed to strengthen trade and investment promotion organizations and private companies in developing countries?
- How might information be supplied on the regulatory regimes of service sectors in the markets of developed and emerging economies of interest to developing-country service exporters?
- Have online databases and electronic meeting places been developed to facilitate the interaction between service suppliers in developing countries and companies in developed markets that may be seeking to outsource work or find partners?
- What is the best way of providing intelligence to services exporters in developing countries on the service markets and export opportunities in developed and emerging economies?

(continued)

Box 2.14 *(continued)*

- What steps have been taken to promote business-to-business dialogue and enhance access to the distribution channels in the service markets of developed and emerging economies?
- What types of assistance, including through private companies, would help developing-country firms enhance quality standards and more easily meet host country certification and licensing requirements?
- What types of assistance exist or should be developed to help developing-country firms and industry associations participate in standard-setting bodies in service industries?
- What type of training and technical assistance would help industry providers, industry associations, or licensing bodies in developing countries participate in and benefit from mutual recognition agreements to facilitate trade and overcome the trade-impairing aspects of regulatory diversity?
- What types of assistance will promote the emergence and existence of coalitions of service industries in developing countries?
- What funding opportunities exist to help small service exporters in developing countries take part in trade missions to developed and emerging economies and to support buying missions in developing and emerging economies by service importers from developed countries?
- How can leading service suppliers in developed and emerging economies be encouraged to share their expertise in service sector research and development, access to finance, quality control, recognition, and so on?
- What steps should be taken to strengthen the ability of small and medium service sector enterprises to finance their own growth and development, including in export markets?
- What special mechanisms might be created to provide funding at affordable interest rates to small and medium service sector enterprises?
- How can financial institutions in developing countries be encouraged to overcome their aversion to lending to service sector firms with limited physical capital and significant intangible assets?

The Challenge of Aid for Trade in Services

The opening of markets in services should be accompanied by a careful combination of competition and regulation. Such a process can present substantial challenges to resource-constrained governments in many developing countries, particularly the least developed countries and small and vulnerable economies. Other aspects of successful service sector reform include progressive liberalization, which is a feature that trade agreements are generally well designed to promote, as well as trade-related capacity building, which involves investments in negotiating and regulatory regimes and institutions (a goal that is acknowledged in the Doha Development Agenda and other negotiation forums).

Combining aid for trade with additional trade and investment liberalization commitments may help advance service negotiations, while addressing the concerns of many developing-country governments and civil society organizations over the extent of asymmetries at the negotiating table. Because of the diversity of the service sectors, any coherence-promoting aid-for-trade package in services requires close cooperation and coordination among multilateral institutions, bilateral donors, and civil society actors, including representatives of the private sector and nongovernmental organizations.

The Doha Development Agenda and ministerial declarations linked to PTAs refer to trade-related technical assistance and capacity building. Without greater effort to give operational meaning to these terms, there may be a risk that the lack, inadequate supply, or inappropriateness of the assistance may frustrate, unduly hold back, or even provide an excuse to renounce reforms and liberalization commitments. To mitigate such a risk, more formal links are necessary between the enhanced engagement in service negotiations by developing countries and the additional assistance from developed countries and multilateral agencies.

This link might lend greater credibility to liberalization and technical assistance programs. Indeed, the development promise of the Doha Round and the ubiquitous calls for coherence in policy making would be well served if future trade agreements entailed tangible provisions and up-front commitments by the leading multilateral and regional lending agencies and bilateral donors to strengthen regulatory institutions. This link has begun to take root at the PTA level, with the recent Economic Partnership Agreement (EPA) between the European Community and the CARIFORUM grouping (box 2.15). The Economic Partnership Agreement is a first attempt at crafting operational aid-for-trade provisions in the service trade and embedding them in a trade agreement. Time will tell whether, how, and to what extent such a novel precedent can be replicated in other PTAs, as well as at the multilateral level.

Box 2.15

Addressing Aid for Trade in Services: The CARIFORUM– European Community Economic Partnership Agreement

The provisions on cooperation in the EPA mark the attempt by the European Union to infuse the agreement with a concrete development dimension.[a] The EPA thus charts new territory at a time when the multilateral community is struggling to give operational meaning to the concept of aid for trade. Part I of the EPA, Trade Partnership for Sustainable Development, provides the umbrella provisions on development. Other issue- and sector-specific development cooperation provisions are contained in all the various parts of the EPA.

Part I of the EPA states that development cooperation takes financial and non-financial forms. Article 7(3) clarifies the relationship between the EPA and the Cotonou Agreement by providing that European Community financing is to be carried out according to the framework of rules and relevant procedures laid out in that agreement, particularly the programming procedures of the European Development Fund, and, within the framework of relevant instruments, through the general budget of the European Union.

The EPA does not feature explicit language on the level of development financing to be made available overall or to be made available for the specific issues and sectors covered by the agreement. This has sparked much criticism throughout the CARIFORUM region over the alleged imbalance of the agreement insofar as the development provisions are somewhat abstract and not legally enforceable, while the liberalization commitments are explicit, legally binding, and enforceable. Responding to this criticism, the Office of Trade Negotiations of the CARICOM Secretariat has cautioned that any perceptions about the practical deficiencies of the EPA with respect to development, development cooperation, and assistance should be tempered by the recognition that the EPA is not the primary vehicle for the achievement of development. Rather, it is a strategic instrument in a range of economic development strategies.

According to the Joint Declaration on Development Cooperation appended to the EPA, a package of €165 million was set aside for the following six years to fund trade-related technical assistance and capacity-building activities identified and ranked in the Caribbean regional indicative plan. This regional package includes an incentive tranche of €32 million for adherence to principles of good governance, democracy, and the rule of law. Of the €165 million, CARIFORUM countries indicated that they intended to devote 30 percent of the regional

(continued)

Box 2.15 *(continued)*

indicative plan and the full amount of the incentive tranche to EPA implementation. Besides the funding for the plan, each CARIFORUM country is to receive funds for a national indicative plan, but must identify two priority projects for the additional funding. The Dominican Republic and Jamaica have announced they will use the financing provided for their respective national plans to implement the EPA.

The development priorities identified in part I of the EPA include the provision of (1) technical assistance to build human, legal, and institutional capacity in the CARIFORUM countries to facilitate compliance with the commitments of the EPA; (2) assistance for capacity building and institution building for fiscal reform; (3) the provision of support measures aimed at promoting private sector and enterprise development; (4) the diversification of CARIFORUM exports of goods and services through investment and the development of new sectors; (5) enhancement of the technological and research capabilities of the CARIFORUM countries to facilitate the adoption of and compliance with internationally recognized sanitary and phytosanitary measures and technical, labor, and environmental standards; (6) the development of CARIFORUM innovation systems; and (7) the development of infrastructure in support of trade.

In the investment, services, and e-commerce provisions of the EPA, the generic cooperation provisions are complemented by a few sector-specific cooperation provisions, the most developed of which are the provisions on the tourism sector. The cooperation activities foreseen are based on the belief that trade-related technical assistance and capacity building are important in complementing the liberalization of services and investment, supporting the CARIFORUM countries in their effort to strengthen their capacity in the supply of services, and facilitating the implementation of scheduled commitments.

Subject to the provisions of article 7, which addresses development financing, the specific cooperation envisaged includes providing support for technical assistance, training, and capacity building to (1) improve the ability of CARIFORUM service suppliers to gather information on and meet the regulations and standards of European Community counterparts, (2) improve the export capacity of local service suppliers, (3) facilitate interaction and dialogue between service suppliers in all parties to the agreement, (4) address needs in quality and standards in those areas in which the CARIFORUM countries have undertaken commitments, (5) develop and implement regulatory regimes for specific services CARIFORUM-wide

(continued)

Box 2.15 *(continued)*

and within the signatory CARIFORUM states, (6) establish mechanisms to promote investment and joint ventures among service suppliers in the parties, and (7) enhance the capacities of investment promotion agencies in CARIFORUM countries.

An additional feature of the development dimension of the EPA is the establishment of a regional development fund. According to article 8(3), the fund will be used to mobilize and channel EPA-related development resources from the European Development Fund and other potential donors. The parties agreed that the CARIFORUM countries are to endeavor to establish the fund within two years of the signature of the agreement. One of the aims of the fund is to increase the speed at which financing is disbursed to the CARIFORUM countries.

Source: Sauvé and Ward 2008.
a. EPA = Economic Partnership Agreement.

The Need for a Tailored Response

The particular characteristics of the service trade and service liberalization add several special features to the aid-for-trade debate. The nontariff nature of the impediments to the service trade means that governments do not forgo fiscal receipts if they engage in service liberalization. Without tariff protection, there is no significant preference-erosion agenda in the service trade, and, hence, there is little need for compensatory payments for countries or regions affected by negotiations based on most favored nation status.

Moreover, the practice of market opening in services—in which the more likely outcome is status quo commitments rather than significant de novo market opening—suggests that far-reaching postliberalization adjustment pressures are generally weaker (or minimal) in most negotiating settings. This implies that discussions of an aid-for-trade response in services can generally be divorced from concerns over the design and adequacy of compensatory financing for those countries that may be adversely affected by market opening, which is a key issue in goods negotiations. Market opening in services may produce a distributional downside, as with liberalization in any sector. Nonetheless, significant new market opening is rarely the norm at the negotiating table.[13] Any opening should, moreover, be properly sequenced, including precommitments to liberalization through GATS article XVIII (additional commitments) to mitigate significant adjustment pressures and ensure that market opening and regulatory strengthening are carried out concurrently.

Adjustment pressures resulting from initiatives in service market opening may also be addressed through an operational emergency safeguard mechanism. Progress in this area of unfinished rule making is desirable, but discussions have tended to become bogged down over repeated and ultimately futile attempts at replicating in a service setting the practices of the General Agreement on Tariffs and Trade.[14]

Devising an Aid for Trade Agenda in Services

Without the need to respond to concerns over preference erosion and significant postnegotiation dislocation pressures, where is additional assistance in services most needed? As Mattoo (2006) has aptly noted, developing countries face two central challenges in undertaking service sector reform. The first is the identification of the elements of economically sound policies, and the second is the discovery of ways to support domestic policies through bilateral, regional, or multilateral negotiations.

To address the deficit in negotiation, enforcement, implementation, and supply-side capacities that the majority of developing countries face in service negotiations, one must take a fresh look at the idea of embedding an aid-for-trade component in service trade agreements. Such a component should target each of the key moments of the negotiating cycle in services (see elsewhere above).

Conclusion

This chapter provides a practical guide to the planning, implementation, and evaluation of a program of service negotiations that may be useful for emerging market and developing economies. A great deal of care is needed to carry out a program of service negotiations. The checklists and illustrative examples we provide will give policy makers background and advice that may lead to an effective and successful negotiating outcome for the service sectors in their countries.

Notes

1. The cost of not opening up or of opening up in a manner that preserves greater policy space—for example, through fewer legally binding commitments or through commitments that favor some forms of entry over others (that is, minority joint ventures versus majority foreign ownership, greenfield

investment versus purchases of existing [national] firms, and so on)—needs to be looked at from various perspectives. These include the impact on access to capital; the resulting investment levels; the nature and extent of contestability in key sectors; the level of competitiveness in particular sectors, in the overall economy, and in export markets; the access to distribution channels; and the capacity to create and innovate.

2. The regional organizations include the Asian Development Bank, the European Commission, the Inter-American Development Bank, the Organization of American States, the United Nations Economic Commission for Latin America and the Caribbean, and the United Nations Economic and Social Commission for Asia and the Pacific. The international organizations include the International Trade Centre, the United Nations Conference on Trade and Development, the World Bank Institute, and the WTO.

3. To assist the process of consultation, the International Trade Centre has published a useful GATS consultation kit, which contains a series of questions organized in three groups: (a) barriers related to the general principles in the GATS, (b) barriers by mode of supply, and (c) possible market access impediments encountered in domestic regulations and the implementation of regulations. These questions may have to be adapted to ensure that all the information needed to assess the impact of service liberalization and formulate requests and offers is captured through the consultation process. See ITC (1999).

4. Services play an important role in the lives of all citizens; so, consumer and user voices should be represented. Transnational nongovernmental organizations may have the resources to provide briefings on general economic and social impacts. However, it is important to ensure that such groups in the domestic economy are also represented and understand the situation of consumers in the particular country. Operators in other sectors of the economy, such as agriculture or manufacturing, are important consumers of services (for example, transportation or financial services). The interests of local manufacturers or producers who could benefit from the domestic liberalization of services, including manufacturers who provide bundled solutions for goods and services, should also be represented.

5. This subsection draws on Sauvé (2008).

6. While all WTO members suffer an information deficit in service negotiations, many developing countries are at a particular disadvantage because they lack the large networks of embassies, the organized industry associations (coalitions of service industries), the foreign affiliates of home-country chambers of commerce, and even the individual company presence in local markets that many developed countries are able to rely on for information. This uneven access to information means that the negotiating requests of some developed-country partners tend to be highly specific and focus on the

progressive elimination or liberalization of sector-specific or horizontal measures that are well identified and ranked. Many developing countries are unlikely to be in a position to make similar types of requests, particularly in the early stages of the request-offer process. This tends to force the latter into a defensive posture and leads to commitment patterns that display considerable precaution, that may be of limited benefit to the development of host nations, and that lack significant commercial value for exporting nations.

7. For a fuller discussion of the potential of developing countries in service exports, see OECD (2003).

8. Some countries, particularly developing countries such as China and India, have shown a tendency to segment the management of PTAs between the goods and the service components, typically focusing on the former first and dealing with services later on.

9. The international organizations with sectoral expertise include the Bank for International Settlements (banking and insurance), the International Organization for Migration (labor mobility), the International Telecommunication Union (telecommunications), the International Trade Centre (private sector development, export promotion), and the World Health Organization (trade and health).

10. This means that small service providers cannot easily compete on the basis of their reputations and must therefore rely heavily on business prospective efforts in target markets so as to make themselves known. This highlights the strong interest expressed by developing countries in opposing restrictions on the temporary entry of business visitors.

11. For many small firms, equity finance is not a viable option. Most small and medium service enterprises thus rely primarily on debt financing to operate and expand their businesses. There is much anecdotal evidence showing that banks are less likely to lend to service firms than to manufacturing enterprises. To some extent, this may derive from the intangible nature of service sector output and the relatively lower value of the physical assets that may serve as collateral.

12. A recent inventory conducted by the European Commission on completed and ongoing technical support initiatives in the CARIFORUM region has found that, of about 200 trade-related technical assistance projects or multiyear programs, only three specifically targeted services. See Chaitoo (2008).

13. An exception is countries seeking accession to the WTO. For a fuller discussion of the level of GATS commitments by newly acceding WTO members, see Roy, Marchetti, and Lim (2007).

14. For a discussion of emergency safeguard measures in the service trade, see Sauvé (2002).

References

AusAID (Australian Agency for International Development). 2007. "Indonesian Ministry of Trade Training Needs Assessment: Supporting the Ministry's Strategic Vision with Training." Report, Technical Assistance Management Facility for Economic Governance Project, February, AusAID, Jakarta.

Cardno. 2009. "EU-China Trade Project: Annual Report 2008." Report, March, Emerging Markets Division, Cardno, Brussels.

Chaitoo, Ramesh. 2008. "Aid for Trade for Services in Small Economies: Some Considerations from the Caribbean." In *Aid for Trade and Development*, ed. Dominique Njinkeu and Hugo Cameron, 300–13. New York: Cambridge University Press.

Chemonics International. 2008. *Indonesia Trade Assistance Project: 2007 Annual Report*. Washington, DC: United States Agency for International Development.

El-Etreby, Ragui. 2008. "Globalization of Services Trade and the Establishment of Industry Coalitions: Conclusions of an Empirical Study." Business and Trade Policy Briefing, April 14, International Trade Centre. http://www.intracen.org/btp/wtn/newsletters/2007/3_2/3_2_services7.htm.

Feketekuty, Geza. 2008. "Appendix: A Guide to Services Negotiations." In *A Handbook of International Trade in Services*, ed. Aaditya Mattoo, Robert M. Stern, and Gianni Zanini, 542–92. Washington, DC: World Bank; New York: Oxford University Press.

Hoekman, Bernard. 2006. "Liberalizing Trade in Services: A Survey." Policy Research Working Paper 4030, World Bank, Washington, DC.

Hoekman, Bernard, and Aaditya Mattoo. 2008. "Services Trade and Growth." Policy Research Working Paper 4461, World Bank, Washington, DC.

ITC (International Trade Centre). 1999. *Business Guide to the General Agreement on Trade in Services*. Geneva: ITC.

Mattoo, Aaditya. 2006. "Services in a Development Round: Proposals for Overcoming Inertia." In *Trade, Doha, and Development: A Window into the Issues*, ed. Richard Newfarmer, 161–74. Washington, DC: World Bank.

OECD (Organisation for Economic Co-operation and Development). 2002. "Managing Request-Offer Negotiations under the GATS." TD/TC/WP/2002(13)/FINAL (June 21), OECD, Paris.

———. 2003. "Opening Up Trade in Services: Opportunities and Gains for Developing Countries." Policy Brief, *OECD Observer* (August), OECD, Paris.

Roy, Martin, Juan Marchetti, and Hoe Lim. 2007. "Services Liberalization in the New Generation of Preferential Trade Agreements (PTAs): How Much Further Than the GATS?" *World Trade Review* 6 (2): 155–92.

Sauvé, Pierre. 2002. "Completing the GATS Framework: Safeguards, Subsidies, and Government Procurement." In *Development, Trade, and the WTO: A Handbook*, ed. Bernard Hoekman, Aaditya Mattoo, and Philip English, 326–35. Washington, DC: World Bank.

———. 2008. "Conducting a Trade-Related Regulatory Audit in Financial Services." Unpublished working paper, International Trade Department, World Bank, Washington, DC.

Sauvé, Pierre, and Natasha Ward. 2008. "The EU-CARIFORUM Economic Partnership Agreement: Assessing the Progress on Services and Investment." NCCR Working Paper 2008/10 (May), NCCR Trade Regulation, Swiss National Centre of Competence in Research, World Trade Institute, Bern.

TFO Canada (Trade Facilitation Office Canada). 2008. "Services 2008." Market Information Papers 23, TFO Canada, Ottawa.

Vonkhorporn, P. 2008. "Preparing for FTA Negotiations: Thailand's Experience." Presentation to the Asian Development Bank–International Institute for Trade and Development course "Trade and Investment in Services," Bangkok, February 13.

CHAPTER 3

The Negotiation and Management of Regulations in the Trade in Services

Sebastián Sáez and Marcel Vaillant

Negotiations on service agreements are on the modern trade agenda. The growing importance of the trade in services has translated into the prominence of services in trade agreements. According to the World Trade Organization (WTO), its members have notified 263 regional trade agreements. Of these, 74 cover the trade in services. Since the entry into force of the WTO in 1995, service agreements have been actively negotiated by developed and developing countries alike. Indeed, North-South and South-South agreements have been the main types of agreements negotiated by WTO members.

Since 1995, all trade agreements involving Japan or the United States have included services. Beginning with the negotiation of its agreements with Mexico in 2000, the European Union has also incorporated services in its negotiations with developing countries, and the trade in services has become an integral part of the Economic Partnership Agreements currently under negotiation by the European Union and the countries of the African, Caribbean, and Pacific group. For example, the Economic Partnership Agreement between the European Community and the countries of the Caribbean Community (CARICOM) and the

Dominican Republic (the CARIFORUM grouping) entered into force in November 2008.

Developing countries face serious resource and administrative constraints in serving their trade interests in negotiations. They are not always equipped to negotiate and implement commitments, particularly in the context of North-South trade agreements. The administrative burden involved is often a serious barrier. One of the problems facing small and medium developing economies, particularly the least developed countries, is a high turnover among public officials and a shortage of resources. This translates into lost expertise and a lack of the information needed to address service negotiations and administer commitments at the multilateral or regional level.

The organization, collection, and administration of information are key elements in a successful strategy to confront these issues. The service regulations management tool (SERET) presented in this chapter provides support for the creation of a database to organize and manage the information needed in trade negotiations.[1] The tool promotes coherence in approaches across agreements and in domestic regulations, and improves the administration and implementation of commitments. It is designed to help countries organize information about existing commitments, laws, and regulations. It facilitates the creation of a country-specific service agreement database and is sufficiently flexible to permit the organization of information in terms of concessions received and commitments adopted.

The SERET database may include information on service sectors, subsectors, and activities committed or received; the type of reservation (market access, national treatment, or other); the mode of supply; the relevant agreements; the laws and regulations in which the measures are contained; and descriptions of the measures. The classification method applied to services is important in SERET (box 3.1).

This chapter discusses the methodology of SERET, as well as the core elements that comprise the tool. The next section describes SERET as a framework for preparing for service trade negotiations and liberalization. The following two sections address the construction of a SERET trade agreement database, first in a positive list, and then in a negative list. The final section concludes.

Understanding Service Regulations: The Basic Components of SERET

Service sectors are heavily regulated. Table 3.1 lists some of the instruments used to regulate selected service sectors, as well as legitimate reasons and

Box 3.1

Sector Classification

Sectoral service commitments are usually specified in trade agreements using the classification of the WTO's General Agreement on Trade in Services (GATS), known as the services sectoral classification list, or the W/120 (WTO 1991), and the United Nations Central Product Classification, known as the CPC or the CPC-provisional (UN 1991).

A detailed correspondence among the CPC-provisional, the W/120, revision 3 of the International Standard Industrial Classification of All Economic Activities, which is known as ISIC 3, and the Extended Balance of Payments Classification, which is known as the EBOPS, has been developed for the purpose of facilitating comparisons.

The correspondence between the CPC-provisional and the W/120 is based on the W/120. It provides correlation at five digits of the CPC. Although most sectors and subsectors are included, there is no available correlation between the W/120 and the CPC in some cases (such as construction or land services).

The correspondence between the CPC-provisional and ISIC 3 has been established by the United Nations. The only sectors excluded from the correlation are land and some nonfinancial intangible assets such as trademarks and copyrights.

Finally, the correspondence between the CPC-provisional and the EBOPS is based on the classification available in annex III of the *Manual on Statistics of International Trade in Services* (UN 2002). An exhaustive correlation has been developed between version 1.0 of the CPC, the W/120, and the EBOPS.

Source: Authors' compilation.

objectives for the regulation. One goal of service liberalization is to eliminate discrimination among similar services and service providers. Certain regulations aim at achieving legitimate policy objectives, but may be burdensome for service providers. Other regulations aim at restricting foreign participation in the market; these regulations are the primary focus of service trade liberalization.

Discrimination against foreign participation may take place at the border or behind the border, and the related measures may benefit some trading partners over others. To address these issues, the most favored nation clause provides that there should be no discrimination among trading partners, while the national treatment clause provides that there should be no discrimination with respect to national or foreign suppliers (table 3.2).

Table 3.1   Reasons, Objectives, and Instruments of Regulation in Selected Service Sectors

Service	Reasons	Objectives	Instruments
Financial	Asymmetry of information	System stability	Financial regulation of the central bank
Professional	Asymmetry of information	Quality of services	Skill requirements, monitoring
Transportation	Economies of scope and safety	Maintaining competitive conditions	Intervention to prevent anticompetitive actions
Telecommunications	Economies of scale, access to public services	Maintaining competitive conditions	Intervention to prevent anticompetitive actions; interconnection conditions
Telecommunications	Network externalities	Avoiding the existence of inefficient small networks	Standardization techniques to facilitate interconnections
Water, electricity, and telecommunications	Distributive aspects	Universal access to public services	Licenses with mandatory universal services; direct transfers to users

Source: Fink and Jansen 2007.

Table 3.2   Discrimination and Rules

Service provider		Location	Rule to address the issue
Benefited	Injured		
Domestic	Foreign	Border	Free trade
		Behind the border	National treatment
Foreign partner	Foreign not partner	Border	Most favored nation
		Behind the border	Most favored nation

Source: Author compilation.

In the trade in goods, protectionism seeks to discriminate against foreign goods at the border. For example, discrimination may be carried out by imposing customs taxes (tariffs) or other measures (nontariff measures) with a potentially equivalent effect at the border. Once the goods cross the border, discrimination may be hidden in domestic laws and regulations.

In the trade in services, many discriminatory measures are applied behind the border, such as restrictions on the establishment of foreign providers in a country or restrictions that otherwise target foreign providers. Market access provisions seek to address restrictions that limit the entry of service suppliers, while the national treatment principle seeks to correct any discrimination in the domestic regulations affecting the trade in services. In addition, the most favored nation clause is applied to prevent discrimination among countries. There are exemptions that allow countries to negotiate trade agreements with a subset of trading partners (bilateral or regional trade agreements).

In the trade in services, regulations may affect the access of suppliers to the market, or they may affect the operations of suppliers (table 3.3). Some of these measures may be discriminatory, or they may affect national and foreign providers in a similar fashion.

The Multilateral Framework: Basic Principles of SERET

Multilateral rules for the trade in services are contained in the GATS (WTO 1993). The agreement is organized into six parts and eight annexes. The first part defines the scope of the application of the agreement. The second part contains the general obligations and rules applicable to the trade in services. The third part deals with specific commitments and the related rules and defines the market access and national treatment conditions accorded by a WTO member to the services and service suppliers of any other member. The fourth through sixth parts address liberalization issues, contain the institutional provisions of the agreement, particularly those on dispute settlement, and create the Council for Trade in Services within the WTO. The annexes deal with specific issues such as most favored nation exemptions, the movement of natural persons, air transportation, telecommunications, and financial services.

The GATS defines the trade in services according to the modes of supply of the services, as follows: (1) crossborder supply, (2) consumption

Table 3.3   Foreign Suppliers and Types of Impact: Discriminatory and Nondiscriminatory Restrictions

Discrimination, impact	Entrance or establishment (examples)	Development of activities (examples)
Nondiscriminatory	Boundaries of two suppliers of mobile telephone services	All retail banking must have staff available to monitor and provide automated teller machine services
Discriminatory	Nationality requirements for senior managers of subsidiary companies; ceiling on shares for investors	Fire and car insurance is subject to additional capital requirements; the crossborder provision of insurance services is subject to price regulation

Source: Hoekman 2006.

abroad, (3) commercial presence, and (4) the movement of natural persons (table 3.4). The agreement includes all services except services supplied in the exercise of governmental authority and air transportation traffic rights and services directly related to the exercise of these traffic rights.

The most favored nation clause is aimed at ensuring nondiscrimination among all services and service suppliers. The clause applies to all measures that affect the trade in services through all modes of supply. However, in contrast to the most favored nation clause in the General Agreement on Tariffs and Trade (GATT), WTO members listed exemptions to the WTO version of the clause in their schedule of commitments before the entry into force of the GATS or in negotiating their accession to the WTO.

There are other general obligations clarified in the GATS that cover governance issues involved in implementing the impartial administration of measures of general application affecting the trade in services, such as transparency and domestic regulations. Additional provisions provide for the development of rules on government procurement, safeguard mechanisms, and subsidies. Although discussions among WTO members have taken place since the entry into force of the GATS, no agreement on rules on these matters has been reached. There are also obligations dealing with balance of payments and current and capital transactions that mirror GATT provisions.

Although the GATS is based on GATT principles, important differences exist. Indeed, the GATS provisions on market access and national treatment reflect the particular characteristics of service transactions. GATT deals mainly, though not exclusively, with market access restrictions

Table 3.4   Modes of Supply and the GATS

Presence of supplier	Other criteria	Mode
Not present in the territory of the member	The service is supplied in the territory of one member from the territory of any other member	1. Crossborder supply
	The service is supplied to a consumer from one member who is in the territory of any other member	2. Consumption abroad
Present in the territory of the member	The service is supplied in the territory of one member through the commercial presence of a supplier from another member	3. Commercial presence
	The service is supplied in the territory of one member, and the supplier from another member is present through a natural person	4. Movement of natural persons

Source: WTO 2001.

at the border, such as tariffs and regulatory measures (nontariff barriers) and discrimination between national products and like foreign products. In contrast, in the GATS, market access restrictions are exclusively domestic regulatory measures.

The GATS defines six types of domestic measures as market access limitations (table 3.5, column 2). If members wish to maintain these limitations, they must list them in their schedules of commitments that are annexed to the GATS. These limitations restrict market access and may also discriminate between national and foreign providers of services. In their schedules, WTO members commit to allow access to and not discriminate against foreign providers in their territories except under the terms and conditions set forth therein. In contrast to GATT, the GATS national treatment provision is not a general obligation. Domestic regulations may imply de jure or de facto discrimination between like foreign and national

Table 3.5   Schedule of GATS Commitments

Mode of supply	Market access (article XVI), types of restriction	National treatment (article XVII), definition	Additional commitments (article XVIII), type of measure
Crossborder supply	Limitations on the number of service suppliers, monopolies, or exclusive service suppliers	Subject to any conditions and exceptions set out therein, each member shall accord to services and service suppliers of any other member, in respect of all measures affecting the supply of services, treatment no less favorable than that it accords to its own like services and service suppliers	Measures affecting the trade in services are not subject to scheduling under articles XVI or XVII, including those regarding qualifications, standards, or licensing matters; such commitments shall be inscribed in a member's schedule
Consumption abroad	Limitations on the value of assets or service transactions		
Commercial presence	Limitations on the number of service operations or the quantity of service output		
Movement of natural persons	Limitations on the number of natural persons that may be employed in a particular service sector. Measures that restrict or require specific types of legal entities through which a service supplier may supply a service. Limitations on the participation of foreign capital		

Source: WTO 1993.

services and service providers. WTO members may list and maintain such discrimination in their GATS schedules (tables 3.5 and 3.6).

Commitments and SERET

In negotiating bilateral or multilateral commitments, countries must take decisions on a number of procedural aspects. First, countries must decide on the service sectors in which commitments will be adopted. Second, they must decide on the modes of supply through which service suppliers will be allowed to provide a service. Third, limitations on market access and national treatment that affect the trade in services must be listed for each mode of supply. This procedure is known as positive listing.

The results of the negotiations are included in the schedules of commitments of members. In these schedules, service sectors, subsectors, and activities, together with any market access and national treatment limitations (also known as restrictions), are listed for all modes of supply.

Under GATT, the disciplines applicable to the trade in goods cover only a share of all possible limitations that affect trade. The GATS widened the coverage of disciplines to include the mode of supplying services through commercial presence and the movement of people (natural persons in the GATS terminology) in the disciplines of nondiscrimination against foreign suppliers both on the border and domestically (table 3.6).

At the multilateral level, trade liberalization has been deeper in the case of goods than in the case of services, but all the barriers involving

Table 3.6   Comparative Coverage of Rules in GATT and the GATS, Market Access Modes

Access barrier		Crossborder, Modes 1, 2		Investment, commercial presence, Mode 3		Movement of people, Mode 4	
		GATT	GATS	GATT	GATS	GATT	GATS
Discrimination against foreigners	Border	MFN	MFN, NT	Covered only if related to CB	MFN, NT	n.c.	MFN, NT
	Domestic	NT	NT, MA, BP	n.c.	NT, MA, BP	n.c.	NT, MA, BP
Barriers to both nationals and foreigners		Little	MA, MS, BP	n.c.	MA, MS, BP	n.c.	n.c.

Source: Author compilation based on Snape (2000).
Note: BP = business practices. CB = crossborder. MA = market access. MFN = most favored nation. MS = market structure. NT = national treatment. n.c. = not covered.

discrimination against foreigners have not been addressed. Trade liberalization in services has addressed a larger set of issues, but has not yet achieved significant results. Thus, the scope of the barriers to trade addressed by the GATS is more general and includes aspects of business practices and market structure, such as the existence of monopolies. However, the process of liberalization in services has faced serious difficulties at the multilateral level, and the difficulties are expected to continue. Some of the difficulties are as follows:

• The positive list negotiations allow all countries (developed and developing) to adopt commitments at a low level of ambition. Thus far, the general commitments represent less than the status quo; the commitments of countries, particularly developing countries, do not necessarily represent the actual level of liberalization of the service sectors in these countries.
• The complexity of the process has meant that the identification of measures, the organization of information, and the selection of activities are imperfect, particularly in many developing countries. The objective of transparency has therefore not been reached.
• The classification of service activities is incomplete and outdated. A more robust system and a greater level of disaggregation are required.

The Liberalization of Services through Preferential Trade Agreements

Countries have been actively engaged in bilateral, regional, and multilateral negotiations on services. The number of preferential trade agreements (PTAs) has accelerated over the last 10 years. Countries pursue bilateral or regional negotiations for several reasons, including, first, the domino effect, that is, the need to reduce the cost of exclusion from trading blocs; second, globalization, which creates the need to raise efficiency and improve access to foreign technologies and investment; third, credibility in that these agreements represent a way to lock in policy reform; and, fourth, foreign policy and security considerations (Hoekman and Kostecki 2001).

PTAs and the GATS have comprehensive objectives in liberalization. However, there are relevant differences between PTAs and the GATS. Thus, PTAs have a more strongly sectoral profile. Liberalization in certain sectors, such as financial services and telecommunications, has been more extensive in PTAs in terms of rules and the elimination of barriers. In some cases, the liberalization accomplished through PTAs has followed a negative list approach whereby countries may exempt or reserve certain activities from selected rules, but must usually justify the exemption or reservation. This is achieved by listing the nonconforming measures that are in force in domestic legislation and that explain the exception.

The aim has been to generate a greater level of liberalization through the PTAs relative to the GATS. However, studies on the evidence have been inconclusive in this regard. This is a complex technical issue, and empirical findings have only begun to emerge (Marconini 2006; Fink and Molinuevo 2007; Roy, Marchetti, and Lim 2007). Nonetheless, some studies have concluded that liberalization has been more substantial under PTAs than under the GATS in terms of sector coverage. In addition, because PTA negotiations seek to bind the existing level of liberalization, the PTAs tend to result in greater liberalization. Moreover, because it is not feasible to implement discriminatory trade liberalization in many service sectors, unlike in the trade in goods, the liberalization effects of preferential service agreements tend to be more consistent with the effects of multilateral liberalization. Finally, the rules of origin are less strict in services than in goods and are therefore less discriminatory in services.

Although PTAs have not necessarily substantively improved the conditions for the provision of services by foreign companies, they have achieved a binding of the status quo, particularly in the case of agreements implementing a negative list approach. In this sense, PTAs have contributed to transparency in the implementation of regulations, as well as ensuring that current conditions for the provision of services are maintained, reducing the uncertainty about eventual reversals.[2]

Service liberalization in developing economies has not yet been associated with a serious effort to open and restructure domestic production. To consolidate a negotiating position in the service sector, a government must clearly define its overall objectives: what are the unilateral objectives to be achieved in service sectors through reform? A government should also make a precise assessment of the domestic regulatory environment—a regulatory audit—for comparison with the requirements of the international standards on national treatment and market access. On this basis, service liberalization, whether through multilateral agreements or PTAs, may become an instrument that facilitates the following:

- The binding of reforms already completed in some sectors, thereby minimizing, through reciprocal agreements, the possibility of protectionist reversals

- Through consolidation, the achievement of improvements in market access in sectors (even in service subsectors) in which a country has offensive (as opposed to defensive) interests
- The promotion of new regulatory reforms that governments have pursued unilaterally, but that, because of domestic obstacles, they have not yet achieved; international negotiations may generate new incentives for the implementation of such reforms

The PTA Service Liberalization Approach

At the bilateral or regional level, three models of service liberalization have been used, as follows: (1) the WTO-GATS model, (2) the North American Free Trade Agreement (NAFTA) model, and (3) the European Union model. Only European Union members have adopted the third model, and it is therefore not addressed in this chapter.[3]

There are two main differences between the WTO-GATS model and the NAFTA model. One difference regards the scheduling of commitments, and the other regards rules. In the case of the scheduling of commitments, the extent of the application of the obligations accorded to specific sectors or service activities is different. In NAFTA and similar agreements, a negative list approach is adopted, meaning that all the provisions of the agreement are applicable unless the country schedules included in the various annexes where the terms, conditions, and limitations are established specify otherwise. The NAFTA provisions on nonconforming measures, that is, measures that violate the agreed provisions, also rely on a ratcheting principle. For example, annex I in NAFTA describes the existing nonconforming measures a country wishes to maintain. If a country modifies a scheduled nonconforming measure by reducing the degree of nonconformity, this change is immediately frozen and represents the new level of commitment. No such provisions exist in the WTO-GATS or similar agreements (Prieto and Stephenson 1999).

In terms of rules, the main differences between the two models are related to provisions on market access and domestic regulations that are not included in NAFTA and local presence, performance requirements, and senior management obligations that are part of NAFTA, but are not specifically addressed in GATS.

Although other types of provisions are common to both agreements, this does not mean that they are similar in scope, as illustrated, for example, by the provisions on transparency and transfers.

The provisions of NAFTA on competition policy rules and their relationship to the trade in services are applied to private companies and to government measures. The disciplines on private companies are general and basically ensure the obligations of the parties to adopt or maintain competition laws and to create authorities responsible for the enforcement of the laws and due process. With regard to government measures, the rules are more detailed and are oriented toward ensuring that no nullification or impairment of benefits takes place through state-owned enterprises or designated monopolies (private or public) and that these entities act in conformity with the general rules and obligations of NAFTA. These obligations are applicable to the service sector if service suppliers enjoy monopoly rights (as a private or public company) or are public enterprises.

In NAFTA, specific commitments are included in annexes following a negative list approach in which countries include the nonconforming measures that affect certain sectors, subsectors, or activities (see above). The original NAFTA text includes annexes indicating the exceptions to certain general rules, including nonconforming measures, nondiscriminatory quantitative restrictions, activities to be regulated in the future, exceptions to the most favored nation clause, and activities reserved to the state.

In general, the first annex lists the nonconforming measures in relation to five rules (national treatment, most favored nation, local presence, performance requirements, and senior management and board of directors). The second annex includes nonconforming measures in relation to future regulations whereby countries maintain their ability to introduce or change nonconforming measures. In the third annex, the nondiscriminatory quantitative restrictions or market restrictions (market access) are listed. The fourth annex deals with exceptions to the most favored nation clause. Finally, the fifth annex lists the activities reserved to the government.

This structure of annexes has evolved in more recent agreements based on the NAFTA model and negative lists. In the most recent agreements, there are only two or three annexes. One is devoted to the nonconforming measures in force, and the other to future nonconforming measures. Nonconforming measures refer to rules on national treatment, market access, most favored nation, local presence, performance requirements, and senior managers and boards of directors. These annexes also tend to be more general, that is, showing horizontal exceptions by sectors, but containing fewer details by subsector and activity. There may also be a third annex dealing with the financial service sector.

Frequently, trade agreements use a mixed scheduling of positive and negative lists. For example, crossborder trade nonconforming measures might be scheduled following a positive list approach, and investment nonconforming measures might be scheduled following a negative list approach. In recent agreements, in contrast to the negative list approach, services subject to market access obligations are specifically listed. Sometimes, a negative list in crossborder transactions and investment is combined with specific commitments in the financial sector (the positive list type), whereby a list of permitted crossborder services is included.

A list of all types of PTAs in services ordered by year of notification to the WTO is presented in table 3A.1 (see annex 3A). The agreements are grouped taking into account the countries or regions that form the hubs of the agreements. Agreements are classified into three types regarding the scheduling approach: negative list (full liberalization, combined with reservations); positive list (specific schedule, mainly with an incremental pattern to achieve substantial liberalization); and a mix of negative and positive list procedures. Finally, the agreements are classified by the level of development of trading partners (North-North, North-South, and South-South). A summary of this information is presented in table 3.7.

Under the GATS (article V), 63 agreements regulating the trade in services have been notified to the WTO. Around three-fifths follow a negative list methodology, and about one-fifth are of the positive list type. The remainder show a mixed pattern. Around three-fourths of the agreements include a developed-country partner. The South-South agreements are concentrated among countries in Latin America and the Caribbean. Globally, the NAFTA-type agreement is the most frequent, representing more than half of the agreements (concentrated among agreements involving Japan, Latin America, Singapore, and the United States).

Service liberalization is characterized by the variety of the sectors and disciplines involved and the high degree of expertise required in each discipline or sector. In addressing the issues encountered in negotiations, governments should take into account the characteristics in sector coverage. The service sectors associated with economic infrastructure have received the most attention so far, including telecommunications, transportation, and financial services. The characteristics common to these sectors are as follows:

- These sectors are paradigmatic of globalization in that an intensive process of technological change has altered the conditions for the trade in the related services at the international level, and this has triggered changes in domestic regulatory regimes.

Table 3.7 PTAs to Achieve Service Liberalization

Totals

Grouping	Negative list				Positive list				Positive and negative lists				Total
	NN	NS	SS	Subtotal	NN	NS	SS	Subtotal	NN	NS	SS	Subtotal	
European Community	8	n.a.	n.a.	8	n.a.	2	n.a.	2	n.a.	1	n.a.	1	11
United States	2	7	n.a.	9	n.a.	1	n.a.	1	n.a.	n.a.	n.a.	n.a.	10
Japan	n.a.	2	n.a.	2	n.a.	1	n.a.	1	1	4	n.a.	5	8
Singapore	1	3	n.a.	4	n.a.	1	n.a.	1	1	1	n.a.	2	7
EFTA	2	1	n.a.	3	1	1	n.a.	2	n.a.	1	n.a.	1	6
Australia–New Zealand	n.a.	n.a.	n.a.	n.a.	1	2	n.a.	3	n.a.	n.a.	n.a.	n.a.	3
Latin America	n.a.	1	12	13	n.a.	n.a.	1	1	n.a.	n.a.	n.a.	n.a.	14
China	n.a.	n.a.	n.a.	n.a.	n.a.	2	1	3	n.a.	n.a.	1	1	4
Total	13	14	12	39	2	10	2	14	2	7	1	10	63

Source: Author compilation based on table 3A.1, annex 3A.

Note: EFTA = European Free Trade Association (Iceland, Liechtenstein, Norway, and Switzerland). NL = negative list. NN = North-North. NS = North-South. PL = positive list. SS = South-South. n.a. = not applicable.

- Services in these sectors are considered extensively in multilateral and preferential negotiations, which means that the international disciplines that affect them have shown a tendency to expand.
- The development of these services has a horizontal impact on economic activity because they are part of the cost function in the vast majority of productive sectors.

From the point of view of technological change, commitments in other infrastructure sectors have also attracted international attention. Among these sectors are the energy sector and environmental services (water, sewerage, and urban sanitation services).

Building SERET: The Positive List Approach

The aim of this and the next section is to provide policy makers with a simple procedure for constructing a database that will allow them to compare, analyze, and negotiate services more effectively at the WTO or other bilateral or regional forums.

In this section, the methodology we use to construct the database for a fictitious developing country grounded on information from the lists of commitments of WTO members is explained. The methodology may be applied for any WTO member or acceding member, and it may be used for any type of agreement that follows the framework, definitions, and scheduling mechanisms (positive list approach) of the GATS.

This chapter explains how the database is built. All supporting files are available on the World Bank Web site (http://go.worldbank.org/DLM9JWE9A0). Users can download and use the files directly and do not need to build their own template, but reading the methodology together with these files is recommended. Please look for this icon (⌘) in the margin, which prompts users to go to the Web site.

Data Sources

In general, a government may begin building a database with its own information and according to its own needs. It may use other sources for raw data such as a country's own services legislation. However, to follow the exact methodology we propose, the data should be arranged to mirror the data structure in the WTO files (schedules). For this example, it is assumed that the country is a WTO member and that the database is being constructed using information available on the WTO Web site.[4]

WTO service schedules for any given country are arranged in a
matrix that lists specific sectors, subsectors, and activities by row and
the respective restrictions and additional information by column
(table 3.8). In terms of structure, the schedules group commitments

Table 3.8   An Example of a Service Schedule

Sector/subsector	Limitations on market access	Limitations on national treatment
Horizontal commitments		
4) Presence of natural persons	4) Unbound except for measures concerning temporary entry and stay of nationals of another member who fall into the categories below	4) Unbound
Sector-specific commitments		
1. Business services		
A. Professional services		
a) Legal services (CPC 861)	1) None 2) None 3) None 4) Unbound except as indicated under horizontal commitments	1) None 2) None 3) None 4) Unbound except as indicated under horizontal commitments
b) Accounting, auditing, and bookkeeping (CPC 862)	1) Unbound except that a foreign service supplier may cede its name to professionals 2) Unbound 3) Participation of nonresidents in juridical persons controlled by nationals is not allowed. A foreign supplier of services shall not use its foreign name, but may cede it to professionals who will constitute and exercise full participation in a new juridical person 4) Unbound except as indicated under horizontal commitments	1) Unbound 2) Unbound 3) Special registration requirements for accountants who wish to audit companies such as financial institutions and savings and loan associations; accounting and auditing standards must be followed 4) Unbound except as indicated under horizontal commitments

Source: Author compilation.
Note: 4) = Mode 4. Other modes and subsectors, for example, a), are similarly indicated.

into two categories: horizontal and specific to a sector. A horizontal commitment applies to the trade in services in all scheduled service sectors unless otherwise specified. A sector-specific commitment applies to the trade in services in a particular sector.

The WTO schedules contain five columns. The first column corresponds to the name of the sector, subsector, or activity classified according to the W/120 classification, for example, 01.A.a, legal services (CPC 861). The second column lists the market access limitations for each sector, subsector, or activity according to each mode of supply, that is, Mode 1: cross-border supply, Mode 2: consumption abroad, Mode 3: commercial presence, and Mode 4: presence of a natural person. The mode is indicated by a number 1 through 4 followed by a closing parenthesis. The third column lists the national treatment limitations following the same approach as in the previous column. The fourth column (additional commitments) lists obligations that are not related to market access or national treatment limitations, but that may affect the trade in services, such as nondiscriminatory licensing requirements. The fifth column (notes) is used for clarifications. (To keep the procedure simple, we have not included the last two columns—columns four and five—in table 3.8 or in the construction of the database; these columns may be included if a user so wishes.)

Because the terms used in a schedule create legally binding commitments, it is important that the terms expressing the presence or absence of limitations on market access and national treatment be uniform and precise. The term *none* is used throughout the schedules to indicate that there are no limitations (market access or national treatment) in a particular mode of supply for a given sector. This corresponds to the highest degree of liberalizing commitment (full commitment) and the lowest degree of unpredictability in the limitations placed on this commitment. However, any relevant limitations listed in the horizontal section of the schedule still apply. In contrast, the term *unbound* is used if a country remains free, in a given sector and mode of supply, to introduce or maintain measures inconsistent with market access or national treatment. This corresponds to the lowest degree of liberalizing commitment and the highest degree of unpredictability in the limitations placed on this commitment. Between these two extremes, many possible options exist, implying that there are specific terms and conditions for market access and national treatment.

Preparatory Steps: Organizing the Data

The methodology we present here consists of a series of steps based on a file that contains commitment information arranged in the WTO data file format.[5] If users begin on the basis of a schedule that has not been downloaded from the WTO Web site, they must adapt the data to fit the structure before following the proposed steps. A typical WTO schedule is shown in table 3.9.

*First step: **Adding the classification.*** The first step is to create the W/120 classification code for each subsector listed and the respective modes of

Table 3.9   First Commitment Schedule Downloaded

Sector/subsector	Limitations on market access	Limitations on national treatment
01.A. Professional services		
b) Accounting, auditing, and bookkeeping services (CPC 862)	1) None	1) None
	2) None	2) None
	3) Foreign investment up to 49 percent of the registered capital of enterprises	3) Foreign accounting and auditing enterprises must use the name of the partners
	4) Unbound, except as indicated in the horizontal section	4) Unbound, except as indicated in the horizontal section
d) Consultancy and technical studies for architecture (CPC 8671)	1) None	1) None
	2) None	2) None
	3) Foreign investment up to 100 percent of the registered capital of enterprises	3) None
	4) Unbound, except as indicated in the horizontal section	4) Unbound, except as indicated in the horizontal section
e) Consultancy and technical services for engineering (CPC 8672)	1) None	1) None
	2) None	2) None
	3) Foreign investment up to 100 percent of the registered capital of enterprises	3) None
	4) Unbound, except as indicated in the horizontal section	4) Unbound, except as indicated in the horizontal section

Source: Author compilation.

supply. Although the WTO schedule classifies sectors and subsectors according to the W/120, one must create a cell with the complete W/120 code to construct the database.[6]

The most rapid method for setting the W/120 code is to create a new variable that combines the sector and subsector codes. Using the fictitious schedule, one inserts a new column between the sector/subsector column and the limitations on market access column. The final text that appears will be the full W/120 code for the accounting, auditing, and bookkeeping services subsector (CPC 862), that is, 01.A.b.

One then creates the W/120 code for the mode of supply of the first subsector. This code must be copied to the other three modes of supply by using the paste as values function. This process must be repeated for all subsectors listed in the schedule. Only then should one proceed to the next step (see table 3.10).

Second step: Using the correspondence table to fill in the blank codes. After one repeats the previous step for all scheduled subsectors, most rows should have a W/120 code. However, some activities will remain without codes because, even if these activities are sorted according to the W/120 classification in the WTO data file, they appear at a level of disaggregation other than the W/120. In these cases, unless the subsector description includes another code (such as a CPC code), it is not possible to assign a W/120 code automatically as in the first step of the methodology. If this is the situation, it is possible to use the correlation table to identify the correspondence between CPC codes and W/120 codes. For instance, in this case, within sector 01.E., rental and leasing services without operators, one finds the activity description, rental of cars without driver (CPC 83101). Because the activity has a CPC code, one may correlate the activity to a W/120 code using the correspondence table.

In cases in which this is not possible (because the subsector or activity corresponds to more than one W/120 code or because there is no CPC number associated with the code), one must assign a W/120 code using one's knowledge of the classifications and the definitions of the subsector or activity. However, it is unlikely that more than a few items will require such an analysis.

Third step: Nesting horizontal commitments. The third step consists of nesting horizontal commitments into specific commitments. This simply means that one adds the horizontal commitments to the specific commitments in each cell containing a specific commitment.

Table 3.10   Pasting the W/120 Code for Each Mode of Supply in the Subsector

Sector/subsector	W/120	Limitations on market access	Limitations on national treatment
01.A. Professional services			
b) Accounting, auditing, and bookkeeping services (CPC 862)	01.A.b.	1) None	1) None
	01.A.b.	2) None	2) None
	01.A.b.	3) Foreign investment up to 49 percent of the registered capital of enterprises	3) Foreign accounting and auditing enterprises must use the name of the partners
	01.A.b.	4) Unbound, except as indicated in the horizontal section	4) Unbound, except as indicated in the horizontal section
d) Consultancy and technical studies for architecture (CPC 8671)	01.A.d.	1) None	1) None
	01.A.d.	2) None	2) None
	01.A.d.	3) Foreign investment up to 100 percent of the registered capital of enterprises	3) None
	01.A.d.	4) Unbound, except as indicated in the horizontal section	4) Unbound, except as indicated in the horizontal section
e) Consultancy and technical services for engineering (CPC 8672)	01.A.e.	1) None	1) None
	01.A.e.	2) None	2) None
	01.A.e.	3) Foreign investment up to 100 percent of the registered capital of enterprises	3) None
	01.A.e.	4) Unbound, except as indicated in the horizontal section	4) Unbound, except as indicated in the horizontal section

Source: Author compilation.

In our example, a horizontal commitment for commercial presence (Mode 3) is listed as follows: foreign investment in activities reserved for nationals must occur through neutral shares, the purchase of which must be quoted on the stock exchange. Because this commitment applies to all listed subsectors, one must paste the text of this horizontal commitment in all cells representing Mode 3 for all listed subsectors (table 3.11).

Table 3.11　Nesting Horizontal Commitments

Sector/subsector	W/120	Limitations on market access	Limitations on national treatment
01.A. Professional services			
b) Accounting, auditing, and bookkeeping services (CPC 862)	01.A.b.	1) None	1) None
	01.A.b.	2) None	2) None
	01.A.b.	3) Foreign investment up to 49 percent of the registered capital of enterprises. Foreign investment in activities reserved for nationals must be through neutral shares, whose purchase must be quoted on the country's stock exchange.	3) Foreign accounting and auditing enterprises must use partners. Foreigners may not acquire direct ownership of land and water in a 50-kilometer strip on the coastline and 100-kilometer strip along the frontiers. Unbound for research and development subsidies and incentives to small service enterprises owned by nationals.
	01.A.b.	4) Unbound, except for measures affecting the entry and temporary stay of natural persons in the following categories: a) persons directly responsible for the sale of a service, and b) persons transferred within the same enterprise, provided they are executives, managers, or specialists. For the purposes of this offer, a) "persons directly responsible for the sale of a service" means persons representing an enterprise that carries on an activity in a country party to the agreement who are temporarily to enter territory (for up to 90 days) in order	4) Unbound, except for measures affecting the categories of natural persons indicated in the market access column. The following activities are reserved for nationals: ship captains, aircraft pilots, ship masters, ships engineers, ships mechanics, crews of ships and aircraft under the flag, airport managers, harbor pilots, customs brokers, and train crews. Subsidies granted to natural persons may be limited to citizens.

(continued)

Table 3.11 Nesting Horizontal Commitments *(continued)*

Sector/subsector	*W/120*	*Limitations on market access*	*Limitations on national treatment*
		to sell or negotiate the sale of a service or conclude agreements for the sale of the service on behalf of the enterprise they represent, provided this does not in any case constitute a direct sale to the general public, and b) "persons transferred within the same enterprise" means employees of an enterprise who have been employed by that enterprise for at least a year before temporary entry into the territory. Stay is for one year, with the option of renewal in order to continue providing services in that enterprise or a subsidiary of that enterprise in accordance with national laws.	

Source: Author compilation.

Fourth step: Sorting commitments according to mode of supply. The fourth step consists of sorting the data by mode of supply. To do this, one must highlight the mode of supply column and sort this column in ascending order.

⌘

Fifth step: Pasting commitments onto the template. Once commitments have been sorted by mode of supply, the data are transferred to a "template" file. This procedure is repeated for all the modes and market access columns as well as for limitations on national treatment.

⌘

Now that the basic structure for the database is ready, it is possible to populate the database directly without following each time all the steps described. The files are readily available for download and can be used directly. In addition, a more friendly visualization of the information is also available, especially for comparison among different agreements. Once the SERET database has been constructed and populated with information on bilateral, regional, or multilateral commitments, we are able to compare those commitments adopted by the country across various agreements.

⌘

In addition to the comparison among commitments adopted according to sector, subsector, or activity, other useful comparisons may be performed. For example, what commitments were adopted according to the type of rule (that is, market access or national treatment)? Also, one may initiate queries to compare commitments across modes of supply. For example, one might determine the activities associated with commitments under crossborder trade (Mode 1) or commercial presence (Mode 3).

The Case of PTAs and the Negative List Approach

This section describes the methodology used to construct a SERET database using information for a country that has negotiated a PTA following a negative list approach. The methodology applies to any country that has followed this approach.

We assume that the fictitious country has engaged in service negotiations using a NAFTA model. In broad terms, this model is characterized by three features that are particularly relevant for the construction of a SERET:

1. The service provisions in the agreements are more complex so that a large number of variables intervene in scheduling commitments beyond only market access and national treatment.

2. The agreements include disciplines on investments (Mode 3) and crossborder trade in services (Modes 1, 2, and 4) in separate chapters.
3. The agreements normally follow a negative list approach in scheduling. This means that, except for the sectors specifically scheduled, all rules and disciplines contained in the agreement are applicable. In addition, the agreements normally include two annexes showing commitments. The first annex covers nonconforming measures, and the second annex covers the sectors, subsectors, or activities on which no commitments have been adopted (the future nonconforming measures).

Taking into consideration these basic features, we present a second option for the construction of the SERET database. The goal is to use bilateral commitments and translate them into the same database format. As in the case of the positive list approach, a pattern is identified as a starting point for the development of a detailed procedure to complete SERET for both horizontal and nonhorizontal (specific) commitments.

Annex 1 and annex 2 in the NAFTA model discuss existing and future nonconforming measures, respectively. The variables in these annexes are sector, which refers to the sector, subsector, or activity with restrictions; obligations concerned, that is, the nature of the restriction applied (national treatment, market access, local presence, most favored nation, performance requirements, or senior management and board of directors); the level of government to which the measure applies (central, subnational, and so on); measures, that is, the legal basis for the restriction; and the description of the measures, including the mode of supply to which it applies (box 3.2).

The second step involves an alteration of the file that is in template form. First, all measures in the prevailing nonconforming measures annex (annex 1) must be placed in the same cell so that the user is eventually able to deal with them together.[7] This is done by copying or cutting the data if one or more measures apply to the same reservation. In lieu of the word *description*, the word *mode* is inserted, and the description is inserted as a new field in the row below (comprising the description of the measures). This step is also carried out for annex 2–type reservations. The aim is to separate the mode field from the description field because both enter into our analysis, but in different ways.

The third step consists of the identification of the specific activities subject to a reservation. Because the information provided in bilateral and regional service agreements is not always associated with a W/120 or a

Box 3.2

Annex 1: Type of Reservation: United States–Chile Free Trade Agreement

Sector:	All sectors
Obligations concerned:	National treatment (article 10.2)
	Most favored nation treatment (article 10.3)
Level of government:	Central
Measures:	22 U.S.C. §§ 2194 and 2198(c)
Description:	Investment

The Overseas Private Investment Corporation insurance and loan guarantees are not available to certain aliens, foreign enterprises, or foreign-controlled domestic enterprises.

Source: Office of the United States Trade Representative, "Chile FTA." Annex 1, "U.S. Measures," page 5. http://www.ustr.gov/sites/default/files/uploads/agreements/fta/chile/asset_upload_file722_4021.pdf.

CPC code, one must add codes to many activities using the activity descriptions as guides and sometimes also the descriptions of the related measures. The correspondence tables may be helpful in this process.

Once the activity has been identified, the user creates a new column corresponding to the W/120 code and repeats the code in each cell of the column that describes the same activity. If a reservation applies to more than one activity, this solves the problem of assigning codes because the reservation may be repeated (copied and pasted) as many times as necessary. For example, in the case of private primary and secondary education, the W/120 codes 05.A. and 05.B are inserted. In contrast, in the case of horizontal measures, the term *horizontal* is inserted as a key word to be used later in the nesting process. An example may be found in those reservations applicable to all sectors.

After all specific reserved activities have been identified and assigned, the empty rows between reservations are eliminated so that one may sort them. Sort by column, which contains the elements of the reservation, and then substitute the obligation concerned and the mode with the corresponding abbreviation according to the worksheet on negative list variables. For instance, level of government is assigned a 1; mode (of supply) is assigned a 1 or a 3; obligation concerned may include national treatment or local presence; and so on. Finally, one picks up the value for each variable to place in the auxiliary negative list file. This procedure is repeated for annex 2–type reservations.

Having completed the table in the auxiliary negative list file, one must now introduce horizontal restrictions in a new column named HR (horizontal restrictions) by copying the restrictions in all the cells.

Once the database is constructed, a country with several bilateral agreements based on the negative list approach and the NAFTA structure can compare the commitments adopted across those agreements.[8] Because of the differences between the structure of obligations and the liberalization approach (negative versus positive), it is not easy to compare results among agreements that are based on the GATS or NAFTA model. The problems arise because of differences in the terms of obligations and liberalization approach. For instance, NAFTA-type agreements contain obligations with regard to performance requirements for investment and prohibition of local presence obligations. Nothing similar is found in the GATS. Our tool does not at this stage resolve this problem and does not provide for a comparison between one and the other. Instead, it provides the option to organize and compare information across agreements based on similar structures and liberalization approaches.

Conclusions

This chapter develops a methodology for building a service regulations management tool (SERET). Originally, one of the motivations for building such an instrument was to provide developing countries with a method for codifying and processing information on the liberalization of the services trade. This objective may be met by analyzing negotiations before any commitments are recorded. However, the tool may also be used to analyze the commitments in force or to construct a domestic database to assess the regulatory regime of a country and propose possible reforms.

The tool is a database on services that covers various types of trade agreements. SERET allows the user to maintain information on service commitments in a convenient format. The goal is to facilitate international comparisons among agreements of similar structure. Specifically, SERET permits comparisons across commitments according to sector, subsector, and activity. Other useful comparisons may also be performed. For example, commitments may be examined according to type of rule, whether market access or national treatment, and according to mode of supply.

The SERET database may be constructed using information on the commitments adopted by the trading partners with which a country is negotiating trade agreements so as to assess the quality and openness of the commitments and compare them to the commitments offered in the negotiations.

SERET is useful because it increases the level of transparency in negotiations on the trade in services. Normally, the global framework for liberalization in the services trade has been established in such a way that the information is contained in a complex text that is not easy to analyze.

This tool is sufficiently flexible to allow countries to accomplish the following:

- Assess their current services regime by uploading the required information into the database
- Populate the database with country commitments at bilateral, multilateral, and regional levels
- Prepare for negotiations by populating the database with information on trading partners, thereby facilitating, for example, comparisons across the offers and concessions provided among trading partners
- Maintain records on a negotiation process by populating the database with information on (1) the current regime of country A, (2) country B requests to country A, (3) country A offers to country B, and (4) actual outcome of the negotiations
- Satisfy numerous other needs identified by the user

Annex 3A Statistics on Service Agreements

Table 3A.1   Service Trade Agreements by Type, Hub Country, Partner, and WTO Notification Year

Hub	Year	Partner	Type
United States (10)	1995	NAFTA	NL
	2002	Jordan	PL
	2003	Chile	NL
		Singapore	NL
	2004	Australia	NL
	2005	Morocco	NL
	2006	Bahrain	NL
		DR-CAFTA[a]	NL
	2009	Peru	NL
		Oman	NL

(continued)

Table 3A.1   Service Trade Agreements by Type, Hub Country, Partner, and WTO Notification Year *(continued)*

Hub	Year	Partner	Type
	1995[b]	Treaty establishing the European Community	FL
		Enlargement 9	FL (NL for transition)
		Enlargement 10	FL (NL for transition)
		Enlargement 12	FL (NL for transition)
		Enlargement 15	FL (NL for transition)
	1996	European Economic Area	FL, NL
	2002	Mexico	PL and NL
	2004	Enlargement 25	FL (NL for transition)
	2005	Chile	PL
	2007	Enlargement 27	FL (NL for transition)
	2008	CARIFORUM	PL
Japan (8)	2002	Singapore	PL and NL
	2005	Mexico	NL
	2006	Malaysia	NL
	2007	Thailand	PL
		Chile	NL and PL
	2008	Philippines	PL and NL
		Indonesia	PL and NL
		Brunei Darussalam	PL and NL
Singapore (7)	2001	New Zealand	PL and NL
	2003	Australia	NL
	2006	Korea, Rep.	NL
		Jordan	PL
	2007	Panama	NL
		India	PL and NL
		Trans-Pacific Strategic Economic Partnership[c]	NL
European Free Trade Association (6)	2002	European Free Trade Association	NL
	2001	Mexico	NL
	2003	Singapore	PL
	2004	Chile	PL and NL
	2006	Korea, Rep.	PL
	2008	Iceland–Faeroe Islands	FL
Australia–New Zealand (3)	1995	Australia–New Zealand (Closer Economic Relations) (services)	PL
	2004	Australia-Thailand	PL
	2005	New Zealand–Thailand	PL

(continued)

Table 3A.1   Service Trade Agreements by Type, Hub Country, Partner, and WTO Notification Year *(continued)*

Hub	Year	Partner	Type
Latin America	1997	Canada-Chile	NL
and the	2001	Panama–El Salvador	NL
Caribbean (14)[d]	2002	Panama-Chile	NL
	2003	CARICOM	FL, PL
	2004	Korea, Rep.–Chile	NL
		Chile–El Salvador	NL
	2005	Guatemala-Mexico	NL
		Mexico-Nicaragua	NL
	2006	El Salvador–Mexico	NL
		Costa Rica–Mexico	NL
		Chile-Mexico	NL
		Mercosur (services)	FL, PL
		Honduras-Mexico	NL
	2008	Chile–Costa Rica	NL
	2003	Macao, China	PL
		Hong Kong, China	PL
	2008	Association of Southeast Asian Nations	PL
		Pakistan-Malaysia	PL and NL
Total		63	

Source: WTO Regional Trade Agreements Database, http://www.wto.org/english/tratop_e/region_e/region_e.htm.
Note: FL = full liberalization. NL = negative list. PL = positive list.
a. DR-CAFTA = five countries of Central America (Costa Rica, El Salvador, Guatemala, Honduras, and Nicaragua), plus the Dominican Republic.
b. CARIFORUM = Caribbean Community (CARICOM: Antigua and Barbuda, The Bahamas, Barbados, Belize, Dominica, Grenada, Guyana, Haiti, Jamaica, Montserrat, St. Kitts and Nevis, St. Lucia, St. Vincent and the Grenadines, Suriname, and Trinidad and Tobago) and the Dominican Republic. Enlargement 9 = Belgium, Denmark, France, Germany, Ireland, Italy, Luxembourg, the Netherlands, and the United Kingdom. Enlargement 10 = previous, plus Greece. Enlargement 12 = previous, plus Portugal and Spain. Enlargement 15 = previous, plus Austria, Finland, and Sweden. Enlargement 25 = previous, plus Czech Republic, Cyprus, Estonia, Latvia, Lithuania, Malta, Poland, Slovak Republic, Slovenia, and Hungary. Enlargement 27 = previous, plus Bulgaria and Romania. European Economic Area = the European Union, plus Iceland, Liechtenstein, and Norway.
c. Brunei Darussalam, Chile, New Zealand, and Singapore.
d. For CARICOM, see note b. Mercosur = Southern Common Market (Argentina, Brazil, Paraguay, and Uruguay).

Notes

1. Files that support the methodology for the construction of the database are available at http://go.worldbank.org/DLM9JWE9A0.

2. A broader discussion of these issues may be found in Mattoo and Sauvé (2008) and Marchetti and Roy (2008).

3. The Treaty of Rome, which was signed in 1958 and contains the key elements of European integration, included a brief, but powerful reference to

the trade in services. The original article 59 prohibited restrictions on the free supply of services within the European Community in respect of nationals of member states who are established in a member state other than the state in which the person resides to whom the services are supplied. The original article 65 states that, as long as restrictions on the free supply of services have not been abolished, each member state is to apply these restrictions, without distinction on grounds of nationality or residence, to all persons who supply services. These provisions apply to services supplied in a temporary manner. Services supplied on a permanent basis are governed by the provisions on the right of establishment set forth in article 52, according to which restrictions on the freedom of establishment of nationals of a member state in the territory of another member state were to be progressively abolished. See Sáez (2005).

4. The commitments of WTO members are available in the WTO Services Database (http://tsdb.wto.org/) and may be downloaded.

5. The steps in building the database are described in detail at http://go.worldbank.org/DLM9JWE9A0.

6. For instance, in the schedule, the b) subsector-accounting, auditing, and bookkeeping services (CPC 862)—is found under sector 01.A., professional services. The W/120 code for this subsector is taken from the combination of the sector and subsector item code, that is, 01.A.b. Although all the information regarding the W/120 code is listed, the full code does not appear in any cell and must therefore be created.

7. All supporting files are available at http://go.worldbank.org/DLM9JWE9A0.

8. Although negative lists and positive lists are normally associated with NAFTA and the GATS respectively, this is not always the case. For instance, the Andean Community adopted a GATS-type agreement using a negative list approach for liberalization.

References

Baldwin, Richard E. 2006a. "Globalization: The Great Unbundling(s)." Working paper, Secretariat, Economic Council of Finland, Prime Minister's Office, Helsinki.

———. 2006b. "Offshoring and Globalisation: What Is New about the New Paradigm?" Working paper, Graduate Institute of International Studies, Geneva.

Dee, Philippa. 2004. "A Compendium of Barriers to Service Trade." Working paper, Crawford School of Economics and Government, College of Asia and the Pacific, Australian National University, Canberra.

Findlay, Christopher C., and Tony Warren, eds. 2000. *Impediments to Trade in Services: Measurement and Policy Implications.* New York: Routledge.

Fink, Carsten, and Marion Jansen. 2007. "Services Provisions in Regional Trade Agreements: Stumbling or Building Blocks for Multilateral Liberalization?" Paper presented at the Conference "Multilateralising Regionalism," Graduate Institute of International Studies and World Trade Organization, Geneva, September 10–12.

Fink, Carsten, and Martín Molinuevo. 2007. *East Asian Free Trade Agreements in Services: Roaring Tigers or Timid Pandas?* Policy Research Paper, Trade Issues in East Asia (June). Washington, DC: Poverty Reduction and Economic Management, East Asia and Pacific Region, World Bank.

Grossman, Gene M., and Esteban Rossi-Hansberg. 2007. "The Rise of Offshoring: It's Not Wine for Cloth Any More." Proceedings 2006: 59–102, Federal Reserve Bank of Kansas City, Kansas City, MO.

Hoekman, Bernard. 1996. "Assessing the General Agreement on Trade in Services." In *The Uruguay Round and the Developing Countries*, ed. Will Martin and L. Alan Winters, 88–124. Washington, DC: World Bank; Cambridge U.K.: Cambridge University Press.

———. 2006: "Liberalizing Trade in Services: A Survey." Policy Research Working Paper 4030, World Bank, Washington, DC.

Hoekman, Bernard, and Michel M. Kostecki. 2001. *The Political Economy of the World Trade System: The WTO and Beyond.* 2nd ed. New York: Oxford University Press.

IMF (International Monetary Fund). 1993. *Balance of Payments Manual.* 5th ed. Washington, DC: Statistics Department, IMF.

Marchetti, Juan A., and Martin Roy. 2008. *Opening Markets for Trade in Services: Countries and Sectors in Bilateral and WTO Negotiations.* Geneva: World Trade Organization; New York: Cambridge University Press.

Marconini, Mario. 2006. "Services in Regional Agreements between Latin American and Developed Countries." Serie Comercio Internacional 77, Division of International Trade and Integration, United Nations Economic Commission for Latin America and the Caribbean, Santiago, Chile.

Mattoo, Aaditya, and Pierre Sauvé. 2008. "Regionalism in Services Trade." In *A Handbook of International Trade in Services*, ed. Aaditya Mattoo, Robert M. Stern, and Gianni Zanini, 221–287. Washington, DC: World Bank; New York: Oxford University Press.

Mattoo, Aaditya, Robert M. Stern, and Gianni Zanini. 2008. *A Handbook of International Trade in Services.* Washington, DC: World Bank; New York: Oxford University Press.

Prieto, Francisco Javier, and Sherry M. Stephenson. 1999. "Multilateral and Regional Liberalization of Trade in Services." In *Trade Rules in the Making: Challenges in Regional and Multilateral Negotiations*, ed. Miguel Rodríguez Mendoza, Patrick Low, and Barbara Kotschwar, 235–60. Washington, DC: Organization of American States and Brookings Institution Press.

Rodríguez Mendoza, Miguel, Patrick Low, and Barbara Kotschwar, eds. 1999. *Trade Rules in the Making: Challenges in Regional and Multilateral Negotiations*. Washington, DC: Organization of American States and Brookings Institution Press.

Roy, Martin, Juan Marchetti, and Hoe Lim. 2007. "Services Liberalization in the New Generation of Preferential Trade Agreements (PTAs): How Much Further Than the GATS?" *World Trade Review* 6 (2): 155–92.

Sáez, Sebastián. 2004. "U.S.-Chile Free Trade Agreement: What Can We Learn?" Unpublished working paper, World Bank, Washington, DC.

———. 2005. "European Union's Bilateral Negotiations in Trade in Services: A Review of the Experience with Developing Countries." Paper presented at the Second Meeting of the Common Market for Eastern and Southern Africa "Technical Working Group of Services Specialists for the Regional Services Assessment," Mauritius, July 11–15.

Sampson, Gary, and Richard Snape. 1985. "Identifying the Issues in Trade in Services." *World Economy* 8 (2): 171–81.

Snape, Richard. 2000. "The WTO Agenda: Next Steps." In *Impediments to Trade in Services: Measurement and Policy Implications*, ed. Christopher C. Findlay and Tony Warren, 358–71. New York: Routledge.

UN (United Nations). 1991. "Provisional Central Product Classification (Provisional CPC)." Document ST/ESA/STAT/SER.M/77, Economic Statistics and Classifications Section, Statistics Division, Department of Economic and Social Affairs, United Nations, New York. http://unstats.un.org/unsd/class/family/family2.asp?Cl=9.

———. 2002. *Manual on Statistics of International Trade in Services*. Statistical Papers, Series M, 86, ST/ESA/STAT/SER.M/86. New York: Statistics Division, Department of Economic and Social Affairs, United Nations.

Warren, Tony. 2000a. "The Identification of Impediments to Trade and Investment in Telecommunications Services." In *Impediments to Trade in Services: Measurement and Policy Implications*, ed. Christopher C. Findlay and Tony Warren, 71–84. New York: Routledge.

———. 2000b. "The Impact on Output of Impediments to Trade and Investment in Telecommunications Services." In *Impediments to Trade in Services: Measurement and Policy Implications*, ed. Christopher C. Findlay and Tony Warren, 85–100. New York: Routledge.

WTO (World Trade Organization). 1991. "Services Sectoral Classification List: Note by the Secretariat." Document MTN.GNS/W/120 (July 10), WTO, Geneva.

———. 1993. "General Agreement on Trade in Services." WTO, Geneva. http://www.wto.org/english/docs_e/legal_e/26-gats.pdf.

———. 2001. "Guidelines for the Scheduling of Specific Commitments under the General Agreement on Trade in Services (GATS)." Document S/L/92 (March 28), Trade in Services, WTO, Geneva.

CHAPTER 4

Liberalization in the Trade in Services: A Negotiation Exercise

Sebastián Sáez and Anna Lanoszka

This chapter presents a negotiation exercise designed for policy makers, trade negotiators, and trade practitioners involved in services. The exercise will help these experts gain a better understanding of the preparatory and negotiating stages of the process leading to the liberalization of the trade in services. The exercise includes a simulation containing a substantive introductory description intended to provide users with easily accessible educational material relevant to the issues under consideration.

The exercise relies on the General Agreement on Trade in Services (GATS) as a framework (WTO 1993). Our choice of this framework reflects the importance of the GATS and its relevance for all developing countries, including countries acceding to the World Trade Organization (WTO). Moreover, the GATS model has also been adapted as the framework for liberalization at the regional level. The European Union uses the GATS as a framework in its negotiations with developing and least developed countries. Among other developing regions, the Southern Common Market and the Association of Southeast Asian Nations have based their integration efforts on GATS provisions and liberalization mechanisms. Because of this, the exercise has a wider application and may be readily adjusted and applied as the bilateral, regional, or multilateral context requires.

The exercise addresses the negotiations in two service sectors in three fictitious countries: logistics services and health services. The aim of the exercise on logistics services is to show negotiators that, although these groups of services present complex negotiating problems, they are connected and are all necessary for the efficient provision of logistics services. For instance, to offer safe cargo handling services, a provider may be required to provide storage and warehousing services. As the exercise demonstrates, such services are often an integral part of the infrastructure and a major determining factor of the competitiveness of countries engaged in increasingly global production and supply networks.

Other areas not directly related to market access and national treatment issues, such as measures on access on competitive, reasonable, and nondiscriminatory terms, are critical components in the provision of logistics services. Among these areas are regulatory matters, such as licensing requirements and procedures, technical standards, and anticompetitive practices, and other procedures and formalities, such as documentation requirements, customs clearance, customs inspection, and electronic processing. The exercise provides negotiators with options and the means to address these areas.

Health services are a regulated sector with particular complexities because of sensitive issues such as domestic health policies. In this case, the exercise emphasizes limitations beyond the measures covered by the market access and national treatment disciplines for all modes of supply and the various categories of service suppliers. These issues are critical for the effective use of trade opportunities. The exercise addresses the definition of health services, the classification of the activities included in the sector, professional accreditation and the recognition of professional titles, and related issues such as timing, transparency, due process, and the burdensomeness of the measures.

The aim of the exercise is to illustrate how the scope of market access and national treatment commitments may be affected by indirect regulations, as well as measures that directly affect health services. For example, domestic regulations on data processing or health insurance regulations may affect the provision of health services. The exercise also deals with other issues that may be relevant to ensure market access, such as mutual recognition and domestic procedures to recognize professional qualifications and address them in the course of negotiations, and it covers ways to generate opportunities for future work. Finally, the exercise provides options for reaching policy objectives that are relevant for this sector, such as wider coverage, universal access, and the role of the public sector in health services.

The Trade Dimension of Logistics Services

Progress in transportation and communication technologies has allowed the fragmentation of production into tasks that may be performed in different locations. Logistics services are a critical infrastructure in the development of the trade in these tasks. The connection among tasks requires an efficient logistics service sector for the production of goods. Logistics services provide the links among tasks performed in different countries. The quality of logistics infrastructure may therefore influence the decisions of firms about the countries in which to open locations, the suppliers to rely on, and the consumer markets to enter (Arvis et al. 2007).

Logistics is defined as "the process of planning, implementing, and controlling the efficient, effective flow and storage of goods, services, and related information from point of origin to point of consumption for the purpose of conforming to customer requirements" (UNCTAD 2006a, 6).

Logistics services were traditionally located inside firms. More recently, logistics services have been outsourced to specialized companies, known as third-party logistics or 3PLs, that offer integrated transportation, warehousing, inventory control, order processing, customs brokerage, and other logistics services. The most frequently outsourced activities are domestic and international transportation, followed by warehousing, customs clearance and brokerage, and forwarding. 3PL firms provide logistics services tailored to the exact needs and specifications of their clients. Although outsourcing has been particularly intense in industrialized countries, companies in developing countries are also beginning to outsource logistics services.

According to some estimates, the logistics industry represents around 14 percent of global gross domestic product (GDP). Furthermore, logistics costs may represent some 10 to 17 percent of GDP in industrialized countries. The logistics industry has grown by around 10 percent per year since the early 1990s. The most rapid growth rates are in 3PL and fourth-party logistics services (companies that coordinate activities among 3PLs), followed by international container shipping and air freight (Memedovic et al. 2008). Government spending on logistics services has been estimated at US$1.4 trillion per year globally, averaging between 2.0 and 2.7 percent of GDP within countries (HP Enterprise Services 2009).

Developing countries are generally ranked low in the logistics perform-ance index, and the high cost of logistics in these countries is a major bar-rier to trade. On average, logistics costs represent 18 percent of firm sales in Latin American countries, reaching 32 percent in Chile and in the countries of the Southern Common Market, or Mercosur (Argentina, Brazil, Paraguay, and Uruguay) (World Bank 2006). In the case of African countries, improvements in logistics services as measured by the logistics performance index provide the greatest benefits relative to any other components of the costs of trade (Portugal-Perez and Wilson 2008). These results have been confirmed for low-income countries in general (Hoekman and Nicita 2008).

However, country income alone does not account for the wide variety of performance levels in logistics services across countries. Thus, for example, Bangladesh, China, the Democratic Republic of Congo, India, Madagascar, the Philippines, South Africa, Thailand, Uganda, and Vietnam are overperformers. This means their scores are higher than expected based solely on income level (figure 4.1). In contrast, Botswana, Croatia, Eritrea, Fiji, Gabon, Greece, Montenegro, Namibia, the Russian Federation, and Slovenia are underperformers, that is, their scores are lower than expected according to income level. These facts, together with a general dispersion in performance within income groups, suggests that policy has a strong influence on logistics sector performance (Arvis et al. 2010).

Figure 4.1   Overperformers and Underperformers: Gross National Income per Capita and the Logistics Performance Index

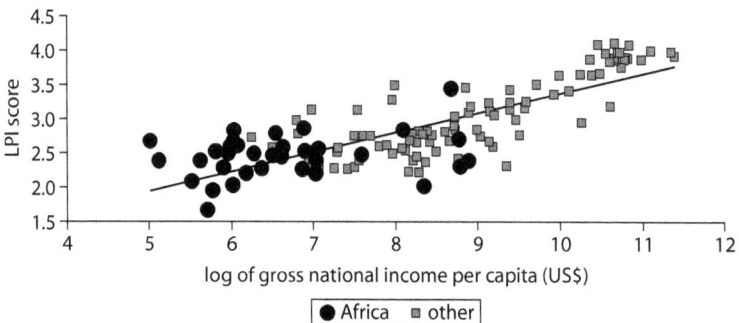

Source: Arvis et al. 2010.
Note: LPI = logistics performance index.

Logistics Service Regulations

Unlike financial, distribution, communication, or professional services, logistics services represent a bundle of service industries. In contrast to these other services, logistics services are thus subject to regulations that are aimed at different service activities. Logistics service providers must therefore deal with larger numbers of regulators who have diverse regulatory objectives and cultures. Moreover, the regulation of logistics services on the basis of the components of the services means that an optimal regulatory regime is difficult to develop.

The providers of financial, telecommunication, or professional services are subject to numerous, complex regulations and compliance requirements. However, the regulations fall under the purview of a single regulator or, in the case of financial industries, a maximum of three regulators who have similar regulatory objectives and approaches. Moreover, although there are different regulatory structures and environments, these sectors, except for financial services, are usually subject to a single licensing requirement.

In contrast, because the development and growth of logistics services have involved diverse service activities to adjust to the demands of clients, the providers of integrated logistics services may be subject to the regulatory regimes of transportation (air, maritime, and land), customs, port, and airport authorities and, in some cases, also to requirements specific to providers of logistics services. They may also be subject to several sets of licensing requirements (de Souza et al. 2007).

One may appreciate the complex structure of the logistics service sector through a classification proposed during the WTO Doha Round negotiations (see also at table 4.2 later in the chapter). According to this classification, three sets of activities are integrated within the sector. The first set of activities is known as core freight logistics services, within which supply chain consulting services and transportation management services are included. These services are offered by the majority of logistics service firms and are often supplied with other logistics services or on a stand-alone basis. Supply chain consulting services deal in global network design and distribution strategies and the determination of transportation needs and appropriate warehouse locations. Supply chain consulting may also cover inventory forecasting and planning, product design strategies, information technology needs assessment, and vendor identification and management. Such specialized services are generally not offered as stand-alone services, but are usually tailored to client needs. Transportation management services deal in storage and warehousing, cargo handling, transport agency services, and customs brokerage (World Bank 2009).

The second set of activities is known as related freight logistics services, within which the transportation services that are integral to the movement of goods throughout the supply chain are included. Most core logistics providers also engage in transportation services. Related freight logistics services may be supplied by firms that use their own equipment and transportation fleets or by firms that act as intermediaries between clients and transportation firms.

Noncore freight logistics services represent the third set of activities. These services cover fleet maintenance and repair, packing services, computer and related services, and management consulting. They are inputs or value added services for the supply chain, but they do not necessarily generate revenue. Thus, the regular maintenance and repair of transport equipment ensure the integrity of transport fleets, although they are not necessarily offered as third-party services to client firms (USITC 2005). Also, while data and message transmission services and other telecommunication services are value added services that are necessary in tracking the movement of goods, they are often integrated with the core freight logistics or related freight logistics services (World Bank 2009).

Restrictions on the Trade in Logistics Services

If they become engaged in international operations, logistics service providers face four groups of constraints embedded in the domestic and international regulations that affect the services they offer. Some of the constraints are common to other service activities, but others are specific to logistics services. Table 4.1 provides concrete examples of the limitations faced by logistics service providers.

One group of constraints is related to market access and discriminatory regulations (involving national treatment violations). Joint venture requirements for foreign investment, rules on the legal entities allowed to provide services, and limitations on foreign ownership affect certain logistics activities such as transportation services. Restrictions on the movement of persons and requirements to employ nationals in certain services also affect the provision of logistics services. These limitations narrow the modes of supply available to providers for the delivery of services.

Another group of constraints is related to the access and use of infrastructure to provide logistics services. In broad terms, there are two types of logistics service providers: asset-based providers and non–asset-based providers. The former use their own equipment and transportation fleets,

Table 4.1 Trade in Logistics Services: Examples of Restrictions

Mode	Market access	National treatment	Access and use	Synchronicity	Other
Crossborder logistics services, including consumption abroad	Maritime: subject to cargo reservation, which requires that a portion of a country's international cargo be transported on national flag vessels Road: regulatory impediments such as limitations on fleet size, equipment usage, and hours of operation		Airlines are subject to domestic laws and regulations that may impede their ability to operate at foreign airports; limited hours of operation at customs facilities; preferred treatment for domestic carriers; security-related rules No coordination between customs and quarantine departments; no automated procedures for items cleared from quarantine; no postclearance process for exports No central processing facility for government agencies	Firms are not permitted to own and operate ground transport equipment In the European Union, shippers are unable to provide uninterrupted crossborder rail transport services between some member countries because passenger transportation has priority over cargo transport, requiring that firms find alternative methods of conveying goods to customers Laws and regulations in some countries require airlines to use third-party providers for ground handling services or prevent airlines from offering such services to other airlines	Border clearance procedures, including customs processing and inspection, are the most frequently reported impediments to the foreign provision of logistics services Customs clearance and inspection are the most time-consuming procedures related to air and maritime cargo transport Customs laws and regulations may be applied inconsistently at different ports in a country

(continued)

127

Table 4.1 Trade in Logistics Services: Examples of Restrictions *(continued)*

Mode	Market access	National treatment	Access and use	Synchronicity	Other
Commercial presence	Brokerage: foreign providers cannot obtain brokerage licenses; citizenship requirements for service providers Cargo reservation: all modes of transportation each require separate brokerage licenses Cabotage: requirement to use local road transportation companies	Licensing requirement for brokers; logistics firms providing multiple services cannot act as customs brokers; maritime and airports require separate brokerage licenses Foreign providers are not permitted to own and operate ground transport fleets and equipment	Ports: the ability of foreign maritime firms to gain adequate access to government-owned port facilities or to provide their own or third-party port-related services is also subject to domestic regulation; in many countries, ports are owned and operated by a government agency, such as a port authority; in some cases, the agency will permit private sector firms to provide maritime auxiliary services, such as cargo handling, storage and warehousing, and container station and depot services; in other cases, the agency will provide all such services itself or designate one or more private sector firms to provide all port-related services		Broker responsible for shipment contents Brokerage companies may not finance services on behalf of customers
Movement of natural persons	Foreign firms: required to hire local residents in countries where they operate	Brokerage: individuals cannot perform services			Lengthy or costly processes to obtain work visas

Source: Author compilation based on USITC 2005.

along with value added logistics services, to provide cargo handling, storage and warehousing, customs brokerage, and supporting and auxiliary transport services. The latter act as intermediaries between clients and asset-based transportation firms, but they may also provide supply chain planning and management, transportation management, warehouse management, and various other services involving information technologies (USITC 2005, de Souza et al. 2007). In both cases, logistics service providers require access to the available infrastructure for their operations. This infrastructure is generally not owned by the service providers and is controlled by other entities. Thus, providers of logistics services require access to ports, airports, and roads that are generally owned and managed by public entities or are licensed to private firms on a nondiscriminatory basis (national treatment and most favored nation treatment). In addition, poor or inadequate road, airport, and port infrastructure may negatively affect the provision of logistics services although this is a consequence of government regulations.

In some cases, conflicts of interest or lack of competition restrict the operations of logistics providers. Facility owners or administrators may also be providers of logistics services, or they may establish requirements for access and service provision by service providers. If this is so, the related terms and conditions on the access to and use of the infrastructure—which may involve preference for domestic suppliers over foreigners, authorization procedures, and applicable competition rules—become critical components of the effective supply of logistics services. The regulatory authority and operations should be separate so as to prevent conflicts of interest.

Egypt offers an example of the types of problems that may arise. According to Ghoneim and Helmy (2007, 15), "the maritime transport sector and its related logistics services suffer from conflicts of interests as port authorities are the owners, regulators and performers, all at once (where they provide services such as pilotage, safety and tugboat, and are owners of companies that provide stevedoring activities)."

In the Philippines, the network of public ports is controlled by the Philippines Ports Authority, which acts as both landlord and regulator. There are small private ports, but they are allowed to handle only their own cargos or, in some cases, third-party cargos, and they cannot compete with the public ports (de Souza et al. 2007).

Likewise, in Uruguay, the port authority is engaged in both port administration and the provision of certain services.

A third group of constraints relates to government regulations. Logistics services are part of a chain that requires the integration and coordination of several services. Government regulations that disrupt this integrated supply chain such as regulations limiting the ability of foreign firms to provide brokerage services, the inefficiency of inbound clearance processes, and regulations allowing foreign investment in warehousing and distribution but not in transportation are also a constraint.

The interruption of the logistics chain by governmental regulations such as the requirement to use domestic operators for certain segments of the chain instead of allowing providers to offer a full range of services affects the integration and coordination that an efficient logistics chain requires.

The fourth group of constraints faced by logistics service providers is related to the management of foreign trade. These constraints may be formal if they arise because of government regulations or informal if they arise because of administrative procedures or unwritten rules. According to the United States International Trade Commission (USITC 2004, 2005) and de Souza et al. (2007), customs procedures and inspections pose the most significant obstacle to 3PL providers. The most pressing constraints are restrictions on the weight and value of shipments and time-consuming documentation requirements, partly because of the lack of electronic data interchange systems. Also included under this category are nontransparent rules, the lack of coordination among the public entities responsible for customs clearances, and burdensome inspection requirements. These constraints are at the core of the trade facilitation agenda that has been the focus of World Bank technical assistance initiatives and research (McLinden et al. 2010).

Logistics Services in the GATS

Since the conclusion of the Uruguay Round, there have been significant changes in logistics services that have been driven by improvements in technology. These improvements have facilitated the interconnection among services that were not previously interacting directly. As a result, for example, the transportation industry has transformed services that used to be provided from port to port and from airport to airport to comprehensive door-to-door services. This transformation has been eased by the growing shift to freight shipping in containers that was first introduced in the mid-1960s and that has enhanced safety and allowed service providers to combine transportation modes in the delivery of goods. The growing reliance on information and communication technologies has also facilitated transactions among consumers and service providers, thus boosting logistics service development (UNCTAD 2006a).

Multilateral rules on the trade in services are contained in the GATS. The GATS is one of the agreements administered by the WTO. Service negotiations are conducted on the basis of the services sectoral classification list, also known as the W/120, which was prepared by the Secretariat of the General Agreement on Tariffs and Trade (WTO 1991). This list aggregates the more elaborate United Nations Provisional Central Product Classification, known as the CPC or the CPC-provisional (UN 1991). Neither the CPC, nor the W/120 have a specific classification for logistics services. Indeed, both systems classify distinct services, such as transportation and distribution, in different sections though they are part of logistics services.

A group of WTO members has developed a proposal for conducting WTO logistics service negotiations, particularly the scheduling of commitments (WTO 2004).[1] The proposal has become a collective request list that defines three pillars for logistics service negotiations (table 4.2; see also elsewhere above). It is nonbinding and may be adopted or not by members to govern national service sectors. Thus, logistics services in the GATS are not part of an integrated framework. Moreover, relevant regulatory issues such as those we identify elsewhere above are not addressed. Bilateral and regional trade agreements have not included the adoption of other, more detailed rules on logistics services.

The first pillar in the collective request list includes core freight logistics services (see elsewhere above). These services are defined as services auxiliary to all modes of transportation (subsection H of the transportation service section in the W/120). Included in this pillar are cargo handling services, storage and warehousing services, transport agency services, and other auxiliary services, among others.

The second pillar covers related freight logistics services (see elsewhere above). It includes all modes of transportation services (subsections A, B, C, and E of section 11 in the W/120, maritime, air, and land transportation services), as well as other, related logistics services such as technical testing and analysis services and courier services. It contains highly politically sensitive services that have also been dealt with separately in the current Doha negotiations such as international maritime services. (A group of WTO members has presented a collective request addressing these particular services.)

The third pillar defines noncore freight logistics services (see elsewhere above). It includes computer and related services, packaging, and

Table 4.2 Freight Logistics Checklist

Core freight logistics services	Related freight logistics services	Noncore freight logistics services
11. H. Services auxiliary to all modes of transport	(1) Freight transport services	The availability and efficiency of the following services are important for the effective operation of freight logistics supply chains; liberalization in these areas would be desirable for a comprehensive offer on logistics: computer and related services, packaging, and management consulting and related services.
a. Cargo handling services	11. A. Maritime transport services	
Container handling services (CPC 7411)	Services identified under maritime transport negotiations	
Other cargo handling (CPC 7419)	11. B. Internal waterways transport services	
	Services identified under maritime transport negotiations	
b. Storage and warehousing services	11. C. Air transport services	
CPC 742, including[a] distribution center services and materials handling and equipment services such as container station and depot services	b. Air freight transport	
	CPC 732 (currently excluded from the GATS subject to the annex on air transport services)	
	c. Rental of aircraft with crew	
	CPC 734 (currently excluded from the GATS subject to the annex on air transport services)	
	11. E. Rail transport services	
	b. Freight transport (CPC 7112)	
c. Transport agency services	11. F. Road transport services	
	b. Freight transport (CPC 7123)	
CPC 748, including[a] customs agency services and load scheduling	c. Rental of commercial vehicles with operator (CPC 7124); without operator (CPC 83102)	
	(2) Other, related logistics services	
	1. F. e. Technical testing and analysis services (CPC 8676	
	2. B. Courier services (CPC 7512)	

d. Other auxiliary services (CPC 749), including[a] through-chain logistics services, reverse logistics, container leasing and rental services

4. A. Commission agent services (CPC 621)

4. B. Wholesale trade services (CPC 622)

4. C. Retailing services (CPC 631, 632, 6111, 6113, 6121), including[a] inventory management of goods, assembling, sorting and grading of goods, breaking bulk, redistribution and delivery services

Other supporting services not covered by 11. H: CPC 743, 7113, 744 (excluding 7441), and 746

Accompanying additional commitments (article XVIII)

1. [The Member] will accept electronic versions of trade administration documents.

2. Service suppliers are entitled to supply listed freight logistics services (from services auxiliary to all modes of transport, freight transport, courier services, and distribution services) in combination, subject to measures necessary to prevent anticompetitive behavior.

3. [The Member] will ensure that various procedures and formalities, such as documentary requirements, customs clearance, customs inspection, and electronic processing, would not be unnecessarily burdensome.

Sources: WTO 2004; "Logistics Services," Collective Requests Database, European Services Forum, http://www.esf.be/new/?page_id=279.

a. These services are not explicitly listed in the official CPC explanatory note. They should be explicitly listed in schedules for clarity.

management consulting and related services. The availability and efficiency of these services are considered essential for the effective provision of logistics services.

The proposal also defines additional commitments that WTO members might undertake and include in schedules, such as the acceptance of electronic documents and measures to prevent anticompetitive practices.

Because there are no internationally agreed definitions or classifications for logistics services, the classifications proposed are being used as a basis for conducting the logistics service negotiation exercise.

Conclusion: Logistics Services

Negotiations on logistics services exhibit special complexities that are not characteristic of other service sectors (table 4.3). First, logistics services consist of sectors ranging from general advisory services to the provision of transport services. These components are all part of a supply chain the proper functioning of which depends on each component. Second, the effective provision of logistics services involves more than the traditional issues of market access and national treatment limitations. It also requires the access to and use of infrastructure that is not necessarily owned by service providers. The terms and conditions for gaining access to and using this infrastructure should also be examined by negotiators. Third, some logistics activities are affected by border management regulations, including customs procedures, that are not related to the direct regulations of these services. This means that negotiation teams should consider the participation of customs and port management experts to ensure that regulations do not nullify or impair the provision of these services.

The Trade Dimension of Health Services

Countries are competing to become key exporters of health services.[2] In particular, the growing phenomenon of health tourism appeals to many developing countries because local clinics providing services for a foreign clientele are flourishing. An increasing number of countries, from Costa Rica to India, South Africa, and Thailand, are offering attractive holiday packages that include surgery, recuperation, and rejuvenation programs. On the demand side, the United States remains the largest consumer of health services worldwide. Deloitte Consulting has estimated that 750,000 Americans went abroad for health care in 2007, and, with a projected annual growth rate of 100 percent from 2007 to 2010, the number is expected to reach 6 million outpatients in 2010 (Deloitte 2008). On

Table 4.3 Logistics Services: Issues in the Development of Negotiating Positions

Horizontal measures	1. Do any measures provide for direct or indirect discrimination against foreign providers through taxation, foreign equity limitations, or land ownership restrictions? 2. What type of government support is offered to providers of logistics services? 3. Do domestic and foreign providers receive state support?
Measures affecting cross-border supply (Mode 1)	1. May nonresidents supply logistics services across the borders? 2. Are there specific logistics services that are restricted in crossborder supply, including because they are considered technically unfeasible? 3. Are there any legal restrictions on the electronic submission of logistics documents? 4. Where and how clearly are any restrictions spelled out? 5. What are the policy reasons behind the restrictions? 6. Are there less trade restrictive means of achieving the same objectives? 7. Are any measures in place to support the enhanced use of information and communication technology to allow improved crossborder supply?
Measures affecting commercial presence (Mode 3)	1. Are foreign suppliers of services required to establish through particular legal procedures? If so, which ones? What is the prescribed legal procedure for joint undertakings? 2. Are there any nationality requirements (for example, with respect to boards of directors)? 3. Are there any prior residency requirements? 4. Are there any foreign equity limitations? 5. Are there any restrictions on the movement of professional, management, and technical personnel? 6. Are there any requirements for the transfer of technology, expertise, management skills? 7. Are there restrictions on the use of the names of international foreign firms? 8. Are established foreign firms subject to specific remittance and foreign exchange restrictions or specific performance requirements, including local content and manufacturing requirements? 9. Where and how clearly are any restrictions spelled out? 10. What are the policy reasons behind the restrictions? 11. Are there less trade restrictive means of achieving the same objectives?

(continued)

Table 4.3   Logistics Services: Issues in the Development of Negotiating Positions *(continued)*

Measures affecting the movement of natural persons (Mode 4)	1. Are there limitations on the number of persons that a logistics firm may transfer as intracorporate transferees?
	2. Are there limitations on the number of persons delinked from Mode 3, such as transport laborers, drivers, or freight handlers?
	3. Are there specific (educational, qualification, licensing) requirements for providers of logistics services?
	4. Are there prior experience or postqualification experience requirements attached to the granting of visas or work permits?
	5. How are entry permits and work permits obtained?
	6. Are there time limitations on the presence of foreign providers of services (for example, duration of stay)?
	7. Is the entry of foreign providers of services subject to economic needs tests?
Measures relating to domestic regulations	1. Is there an adequate legal framework that is supportive of trade in logistics services and that recognizes the legal effects and validity of electronic data messages and transactions?
	2. Do provisions in domestic law protect service providers from corruption, theft, and accidents?
	3. Are there any qualification or licensing requirements or procedures or technical standards that affect (the trade in) logistics services?
Issues relating to technical and security standards, professional qualifications, and so on	1. Are technical, industry, and security standards being implemented?
	2. Are these standards transparent and nondiscriminatory?
	3. Is there an independent body monitoring the implementation of these standards?
	4. Is there widespread data security in the country?
	5. What conditions must foreign providers of services fulfill to meet the requirements of the mutual recognition agreements to which the host country is a party?
	6. Do foreign providers of services need to be locally established to be eligible for participation in mutual recognition agreements?
Universal access	1. Which universal service regulations apply?
	2. May the government impose obligations on service providers concerning the development of logistics service infrastructure?
	3. What measures or mechanisms are in place for the achievement of public service obligations?
	4. Are these measures objective and transparent?
	5. Are foreign suppliers of services subject to different conditions relative to domestic suppliers in terms of public service obligations?

Implementation of article IV; contributions to competitive developing-country services and exports	1. Are there any policies or initiatives to improve the quality and competitiveness of logistics services in developing countries (including through encouragement for the transfer of technology, joint ventures, and so on)? 2. Do commitments exist or are commitments being offered in modes of export of interest to developing countries? 3. Might one envisage the use of additional article XVIII commitments related to logistics as a tool for implementing article IV?
Issues relating to the adequacy of technology, equipment, and so on	1. Is there adequate information and communication technology to allow information to be exchanged, contracts to be entered into, and goods to be tracked during transit? 2. Is there both public and private investment in the related technology and infrastructure? 3. Is there a sufficient number of trained personnel to deal with information and communication technology and container cargo efficiently? 4. Are there public policies aimed at improving the overall quality of the technology in the country? 5. Are there any restrictions on the temporary admission of the equipment needed to carry out services in a foreign market or on the maintenance of such equipment?
Competition issues	1. Are there sectoral exemptions to competition law in the importing country that affect the conditions for competition in logistics service markets? 2. Is there competition among the domestic providers of logistics services? 3. Are contracts awarded in a transparent manner (for example, by using tender procedures)? 4. Are any of the logistics services offered by providers within the reserved domain of a state monopoly (for example, a postal monopoly)? 5. Do any licenses grant exclusive rights? 6. How does the competition law define and deal with instances of the abuse of monopoly power? Cartels? 7. Is there both public and private participation in ports? 8. Is the ownership of certain transport facilities reserved to the public sector?
Preferential liberalization measures, most favored nation obligation	1. Are there any preferential agreements, including in the regional context, affecting the supply of any logistics services? 2. Do these preferential arrangements apply to the movement of natural persons? 3. Do any preferential access measures favor developing countries?

Source: Author adaptation for logistics services based on UNCTAD (2006b), annex.

the supply side, in 2008, more than 400,000 non–United States residents sought care in the United States and spent almost US$5 billion for health services; there were 300,000 in Malaysia, 410,000 in Singapore, 450,000 in India, and 1.2 million in Thailand (Deloitte 2008). The motives for the crossborder movement of patients vary considerably, however, and not all countries are competing in the same market segments. There is thus a case for specialization on the basis of resources and trade opportunities.

Medical tourism has received significant media attention, but the trade in health services is not limited to the crossborder movement of patients, which represents only one of the four possible modes of service delivery identified by the GATS (Mode 2). The other modes are the temporary movement of health professionals to deliver services across borders (Mode 4), for example, the crossborder movement of doctors and nurses; foreign establishment (Mode 3), for example, the opening of a branch abroad by a clinic; and the crossborder provision of health services through technological means (Mode 1), for example, telemedicine. Other services and goods are also traded at the margin of health services; it is a common characteristic of many services that they enable trade in other sectors. Other examples of the modes are indicated in table 4.4.

The trade in health services has potentially significant effects on the availability of these services, the quality of health systems, and the health of populations in exporting and importing countries. The effects of the trade in health services vary considerably from one mode of delivery to another, and imports often appear more important than exports in improving a domestic health system. An excessive enthusiasm for medical tourism that is not backed by serious business plans or coherent government policies may result in low returns on investment, lead to frustrated expectations, and prejudice the local supply of health services. Not all countries have a comparative advantage in the health service trade. While a carefully designed trade strategy in the health sector may have significant and positive spillover effects on the domestic supply of and access to health services (in addition to the positive impacts on global trade), a poorly designed strategy may divert already scarce resources from people in need in developing countries.

Health is not merely a commodity, and health care is not merely a service: they are public goods. The trade in health services may contribute directly to reaching or missing—if the negative effects prevail—the health-related Millennium Development Goals.[3] Trade objectives in the health sector should be compatible with other legitimate social objectives (for example, universal access).

Table 4.4 The Modes of Trade in the Health Sector

Mode	Health services	Ancillary services	Associated goods
Mode 1, crossborder supply	Telemedicine, including diagnostics, radiology	Remote medical education and training Medical transcription, back-office services Medical research tools and databases Medical insurance	Health care equipment Drugs Medical waste Prosthesis
Mode 2, consumption abroad	Medical tourism, that is, voluntary travel to receive medical treatment abroad Medically assisted living in residences for retirees Expatriates seeking care in countries of residence Emergency cases (for example, accidents abroad)	All activities associated with health tourism (transport, hotel, restaurant, paramedical, local purchases, and so on) Local medical education and training among foreign nationals	
Mode 3, commercial presence	Foreign participation or ownership of hospitals, clinics, or medical facilities (for example, capital investments, technology tie-ins, collaborative ventures)	Foreign-sponsored education or training centers Foreign-sponsored medical research facilities	
Mode 4, presence of natural persons	Movement of doctors and health personnel for the purpose of commercial medical practice	Movement of doctors and health personnel for other purposes (for example, education or training)	

Source: World Bank staff.

Health is also a highly regulated profession, and this is so for legitimate purposes: even more than other professional services, medicine is characterized by the asymmetry of information between service providers (doctors trained in the practice of medicine) and consumers (the patients). The regulation of the health sector is necessary to protect patients against malpractice. Therefore, the promotion of trade in the health sector is not focused on deregulation, but on more effective regulation and, sometimes, on more regulation, for example, to adopt higher-quality standards in hospitals and clinics. Similarly, the promotion of trade is not focused on challenging the public health sector, which often plays a crucial role in the supply of health services and medical education, but on designing efficient services within a more competitive environment. Experience shows that public involvement is often necessary for the success of export promotion strategies in the health sector. Nonetheless, private investment, including foreign investment, remains a crucial factor in success, particularly if public resources are lacking to maintain an efficient health system.

The sustainability of public health insurance schemes, the aging of populations, and related supply bottlenecks in health systems are among the drivers of frustration and outbound medical tourism in the North. Most developing countries face far more crucial health issues, such as critically low availability of medical services and poor quality in infrastructure and services, that, combined with other factors, result in poor public health and higher mortality rates. In all these countries, the trade in health services should be considered not only as a source of income in the balance of payments, but primarily as a means to remedy shortages and improve domestic health systems. The main challenge is therefore to find adequate accompanying policies that are able to maximize the positive domestic spillovers and minimize the negative domestic spillovers of the trade in health services.

The focus of the media and of many expert studies has been on North-South trade (for example, the movement of patients) or South-North trade (for example, the movement of doctors and nurses). The potential of South-South trade has often been ignored or neglected, in sharp contrast with the reality in trade. In Tunisia, for example, Libyans represent more than 80 percent of the foreign medical patients; similarly, more than 80 percent of the Omani patients treated abroad have been treated in India. There is justification for greater cooperation in the South. This may involve the creation of regional health centers of excellence (for medical education or treatment) to share the cost of medical education and infrastructure and reach a critical size to offset the cost of investment in technology.

When Should Health Services Be Liberalized under the GATS?

The GATS is silent on whether and to what extent the financing and delivery of health services should be privatized in a country.[4] The GATS only deals with the treatment of foreigners, not nationals, and the GATS is silent on national debates on allowing the private sector to play a role in the health care system.

Once the decision to privatize has been made, the GATS becomes useful. It may then assist in addressing the desire to increase the efficiency of national private sector providers by exposing them to competition, the use of foreign suppliers to meet key shortages in the short to medium term, the desire to gain access to new technologies or skills that may not be available through national suppliers, and the desire to increase the facilities and services available to health care consumers despite the lack of capacity among domestic suppliers. Equal consideration must also be given to determining how to ensure the quality of foreign providers and the impact of foreign suppliers on local suppliers and on the local health care system.

How Do Commitments Made under the GATS Impact a Country's Health Policy?

Liberalizing commitments made under the GATS apply to profit-oriented health services, and they therefore concern private providers. The GATS excludes services provided through the exercise of governmental authority as long as such services are not provided on a commercial basis or in competition with other services.

Is the Main Focus the Commitments on Market Access and National Treatment?

The commitments on market access and national treatment are not always sufficient to allow foreign providers of services to supply a market. Indeed, if the country that imports the service does not recognize the qualifications of foreign providers, the value of any market access that has been granted is neutralized. The recognition of qualifications is a crucial element in the provision of health services. This is one area in which the government must protect public health and information asymmetries by establishing the qualifications required for the provision of services. The nursing and medical professions are particularly affected by the criteria applied in the recognition of qualifications. Article VII of the GATS provides that members may enter into mutual recognition agreements enabling them to certify the education or experience obtained, the requirements met, or the licenses or other documents issued in one or several other countries (Blouin, Drager, and Smith 2006).

Additional Benefits

Enhancing the international trade in health services may have positive impacts in terms of the availability of capital for infrastructure, new knowledge, and new technology. To this extent, governments can introduce measures to ensure that these additional resources are harnessed to benefit national health systems. Examples of such measures include the following (Blouin, Drager, and Smith 2006):

- Mode 1, crossborder supply: National governments may adopt international cooperative agreements to facilitate telemedicine and information sharing on the health services offered through the Internet.
- Mode 2, consumption abroad: Policy makers may consider various measures to ensure that the additional incomes from foreign patients are harnessed to benefit the national health system more generally. For instance, the government may restrict the provision of health services to foreigners to private clinics, tax the profits of these clinics, and earmark the revenue for the public health system. If services are provided to foreign patients by public hospitals, administrative mechanisms may be put in place to ensure that the additional revenue generated from the treatment of foreign patients subsidizes the provision of services to other patients (which is often the case in education).
- Mode 3, commercial presence: To take advantage of new services offered by foreign providers and make these services available to all income groups, governments may target individual patients and provide subsidies or vouchers for types of treatments that are not available in the public system, but that are available in private foreign-owned establishments. The additional resources generated by foreign investors may be harnessed to subsidize the public health system by taxing the profits of foreign providers.
- Mode 4, presence of natural persons: In addition to the improvement of skills, one of the key benefits for developing countries of health service exports through Mode 4 is the potential for remittances. Ways should be sought to harness the private flows of remittances for the development of the health system.

Health Services: Issues to Consider in Developing Negotiating Positions

What regulatory issues should be considered? Are any GATS disciplines related to local regulatory methods (Blouin, Drager, and Smith 2006)?

Foreign suppliers only gain local access to provide services that are permitted in a country. Thus, for example, a commitment on Mode 3 market access for foreign clinics does not enable these clinics to provide services that are forbidden by law (table 4.5).

Commitments do not interfere with the ability of WTO members to regulate health services. Foreign entrants to the market remain subject to the national regulatory framework. GATS commitments also allow a country to impose stricter regulations or special conditions on foreign suppliers provided a national treatment limitation is scheduled.

Where no commitments are made for a sector, only the general obligations apply (for example, most favored nation and transparency). Where commitments are made, additional procedural obligations apply (related to transparency, the administration of measures, decisions regarding authorizations to supply a service, and recognition).

Regulatory measures on qualification and licensing requirements and procedures and on technical standards that are nondiscriminatory and that are not market access restrictions may be subject to disciplines developed under article VI.4 of the GATS, which concerns domestic regulation.

WTO members may also make commitments to apply good regulatory practices either for a particular sector or across all sectors (for example, providing all national and foreign suppliers with the opportunity to comment on new regulations before they are introduced).

WTO members are free to recognize the qualifications of some members and not others. However, they must notify any recognition agreements they are negotiating and give other interested WTO members the opportunity to prove that they meet the same standards. If a commitment to provide access to health service professionals has been made, adequate procedures must be available to verify the competence of these professionals.

Conclusions: Health Services

Negotiations on health services involve complexities that are similar to the complexities involved in negotiations on other service activities with a significant impact on social development, such as education and social security. First, in liberalizing health services, governments must ensure that the level of the access to the services is improved or, at least, maintained. This requires that government policies not be negatively affected by greater liberalization. Second, liberalization in this sector means that important decisions must be adopted by governments on the role of the public and private sectors as regulators and service providers. Third,

Table 4.5 Health Service Trade: Issues to Consider in Developing Negotiating Positions

Horizontal measures	1. Do any measures directly or indirectly discriminate against foreign providers or impose market access limitations on foreign providers?
	2. What is the nature of the government involvement in the sector: regulator, provider, or a combination?
	3. Do domestic and foreign providers receive state support?
Measures affecting cross-border supply (Mode 1)	1. Can nonresidents supply health services from across the borders?
	2. Are specific activities restricted (including because they are considered technically unfeasible) in terms of crossborder supply?
	3. Are there legal restrictions on the electronic submission of information documentation (for example, for reasons of data protection or other reasons)?
	4. Where and how clearly are restrictions spelled out?
	5. What are the policy reasons behind the restrictions?
	6. Are there less trade restrictive means of achieving the same objectives?
	7. Do any measures support enhanced applications of information and communication technology so as to allow improved crossborder supply?
Measures affecting commercial presence (Mode 3)	1. Are foreign suppliers of services allowed to establish a commercial presence? Are they required to establish through particular legal procedures? If so, which ones? What is the prescribed legal procedure for a joint undertaking?
	2. Are there any nationality requirements regarding management, the number of workers, or boards of directors?
	3. Are there any prior residency requirements?
	4. Are there any foreign equity limitations?
	5. Are there any restrictions on the movement of professional, management, or technical personnel?
	6. Are there any requirements for the transfer of technology, expertise, management skills?
	7. Are there restrictions on the use of the names of international foreign firms?

8. Are established foreign firms subject to specific performance requirements, including local content and manufacturing requirements, and remittance and foreign exchange restrictions?
9. Where and how clearly are restrictions spelled out?
10. What are the policy reasons behind the restrictions?
11. Are there less trade restrictive means of achieving the same objectives?

Measures affecting the movement of natural persons (Mode 4)	1. Are there limitations on the number of persons that may be transferred as intracorporate transferees?
	2. Are there limitations on the number of persons delinked from Mode 3, such as doctors or nurses?
	3. Are there specific requirements for providers (educational, qualification, licensing)?
	4. Are there prior experience or postqualification experience requirements attached to the issuance of visas or work permits?
	5. How are entry permits and work permits obtained?
	6. Are there time limitations on the presence of foreign providers of services (for example, duration of stay)?
	7. Do measures limit the participation of foreign providers in the public sector?
	8. Is the entry of foreign providers of services subject to economic needs tests?
Measures relating to domestic regulations	1. Is there an adequate legal framework supportive of the trade in health services?
	2. Are there provisions in domestic law that protect service providers from corruption, theft, and accidents?
	3. Are there any qualification or licensing requirements or procedures or technical standards that affect (the trade in) health services?
Issues relating to technical and security standards, professional qualifications, and so on	1. Are technical, industry, and security standards implemented?
	2. Are these standards transparent and nondiscriminatory?
	3. Is there an independent body monitoring the implementation of these standards?
	4. Is there widespread data security in the country?
	5. What conditions must foreign providers of services fulfill to meet the requirements of existing mutual recognition agreements to which the host country is a party?
	6. Must foreign providers of services be locally established to participate in mutual recognition agreements?

(continued)

145

Table 4.5 Health Service Trade: Issues to Consider in Developing Negotiating Positions *(continued)*

Universal access	1. What universal service regulations apply? 2. May the government impose obligations relating to universal access on service providers? 3. What measures or mechanisms are in place for the achievement of public service obligations? 4. Are these measures objective and transparent? 5. Are foreign suppliers of services subject to different conditions relative to domestic suppliers in relation to public service obligations?
Issues relating to adequate technology, equipment, and so on	1. Are there any restrictions on the temporary admission of the equipment necessary to provide services?
Competition issues	1. Are there sectoral exemptions to competition law that affect the conditions of competition? What is the role of professional bodies in determining the conditions of competition? 2. Are there limitations on competition between domestic service providers and foreigners? 3. Do any licenses grant exclusive rights?
Preferential liberalization measures, most favored nation obligation	1. Do any preferential agreements, including in the regional context, affect the supply of any health services? 2. Do these preferential arrangements apply to the movement of natural persons? 3. Do any preferential access measures favor developing countries?

Source: Author adaptation for logistics services based on UNCTAD (2006b), annex.

different options may be pursued by governments according to policy objectives. For instance, a government may open the provision of health services to foreign doctors and nurses and maintain the provision of these services as public services. A government may also wish to open health services to private investors, while maintaining nondiscriminatory universal access requirements to ensure broad policy objectives. A government may encourage the provision of health services to foreign consumers (patients) as a means to create profitable activities for domestic doctors. Fourth, service agreement architectures provide for a range of options in addressing liberalization in health services and ensuring consistency with the social objectives of governments.

Trade in Services: A Negotiation Exercise

Learning Objectives
After this simulation exercise has been completed, the participants are expected to understand the complexities of the liberalization of logistics and health services and to have enhanced their technical skills with respect to negotiations within the framework of the WTO, the GATS, and other, regional agreements.[5]

The simulation is intended to be an engaging educational experience. The final outcome is anticipated to be a win-win scenario. Given the number of ways the simulation may unfold, the idea is not to force participants to reach a particular best possible solution, but rather to provide them with an opportunity to perfect their negotiating and technical skills in the area of service liberalization.

The Length of the Simulation and the Number of Participants
The simulation is designed to run from three to five days, depending on the level of expertise and the declared needs of the participants. The optimum number of participants is 24 (that is, 8 for each of the three countries involved: 4 representing government officials and 4 representing interested private stakeholders). However, the simulation is designed to be sufficiently flexible to accommodate between 18 and 30 participants successfully.

This comprehensive exercise is intended to be used as part of a broader course on the trade in services. It is designed to accommodate participants with considerable knowledge of negotiations and services, as well as participants who are in the process of learning or sharpening skills.

Participants who wish to develop their knowledge or practice their negotiating skills will find this exercise especially useful. The exercise focuses on two sectors, logistics and health, to highlight issues that relate to particular sectors, but remains grounded within the general framework of service negotiations.

It is recommended that the exercise be fully presented and explained at the beginning of a course on the trade in services so that participants may become familiar with it while they are learning the required knowledge and may apply their new knowledge directly to the sectors in the exercise. Discussions and clarifications must be pursued as the course progresses. The last part of the course should concentrate on the exercise. This calls for intense interaction among participants, instructors, and their colleagues.

Instructions for the First Part of the Exercise

The aim of the first part of the exercise. Each delegation or country team, led by the participants representing government officials, should prepare a negotiating position for the plurilateral stage of the negotiations on the liberalization of the trade in services. The negotiating position will focus on sectors related to health services and logistics services, but, in their negotiation strategies, participants may also wish to use other sectors or include other issues in the course of the negotiations. The framework of the negotiations is the GATS or GATS-type agreements (see chapter 3 for a discussion on the differences between the GATS model and other models of service liberalization). There are three countries involved in the negotiations, A, B, and C.[6] Each of the three country delegations is expected to prepare its position as a team. The teams consist of government officials working in consultation with interested private stakeholders.

Concluding the first part of the exercise. To conclude the first part of the exercise, each negotiating country team should prepare the following documents:

1. A negotiating position paper drafted in consultation with the private stakeholders. The document is to be given to the instructor. The document should include the following:

   - The concerns of each country with regard to the negotiations
   - The country goals in the negotiations
   - A list of the offensive interest(s) of the country; these are determined through consultations

- A list of the defensive interest(s) of the country, including an expla-
  nation of each point
- An ideal schedule, which represents the most advantageous negotiating outcome for the participating country
- A paper describing and specifying the general regulatory reform that
  may be necessary as a result of the negotiations; the paper should
  identify the role of trade policy in the achievement of the objectives
  of reform

This document will allow the instructor(s) to assess the performance
of the team according to initial objectives and final results.

2. A proposal representing the country's initial offer. The proposal must
   take the form of a revised schedule of the country's specific commitments.[7] It will be forwarded to every government delegation in the
   plurilateral group.
3. Two individual requests directed at every trading partner in the plurilateral group.

The preparation of the documents requires the following:

- Each country team should nominate a chairperson to represent the
  government.
- The chairperson becomes the team's chief negotiator.
- Allow all the government and private stakeholders sufficient time to
  read the confidential set of priorities prepared by the leading trade
  and development experts in each country.
- Carefully read the descriptions of the three countries.
- Carefully analyze all three schedules of specific commitments as a
  starting step in negotiations.
- Start to evaluate your country's priorities with respect to services.
- Each country team should elaborate an overall reform strategy in the
  context of service liberalization.
- Rank issues in terms of importance.
- Assess the relevant domestic conditions and priorities and formulate a
  negotiating position in consultation with relevant stakeholders.
- Identify starting offers for each sector in the scenario.
- As a team, formulate the country's negotiating position.
- As a team, prepare a proposal and distribute it to the other negotiat-
  ing teams in the group.
- As a team, prepare an individual request for each of the other trading
  partners in the group.

Descriptions of the Three Negotiating Countries

This exercise includes the countries A, B, and C. These three countries are members of a multilateral trade organization, which is an intergovernmental organization. They are about to engage in negotiations aimed at advancing the liberalization of the international trade in services. For the purpose of the exercise, this plurilateral stage of negotiations will focus on sectors related to health services and logistics services. All countries are fictitious and are not intended to resemble real countries. Each country is represented by a delegation consisting of government officials. In addition, several representatives of relevant stakeholders are participating to monitor the negotiations. These stakeholders actively engage in consultations with the government officials to ensure the transparency of the decision-making process and the availability of well-informed assessments of the proposals and offers presented at the negotiating table.

Country A.

Population: 50 million
GDP per capita in 2007: US$38,000
Annual average economic growth in 2004–07: 3 percent

Country A's negotiating team includes government officials, as follows:

- Representative(s) of the Ministry of Trade
- Representative(s) of the Ministry of Transport
- Representative(s) of the Ministry of Health and Welfare
- Representative(s) of the Ministry of Finance

Stakeholders observing the negotiation process include the following:

- Representative(s) of Country A's Alliance of City Councils
- Representative(s) of the Service Sector Coalition
- Representative(s) of the Association of Professionals

Relevant economic data—Country A's per capita GDP, at US$38,000, is among the world's highest. Country A is a large developed country with access to the sea. Its trade policy has traditionally been outward looking, which helps explain Country A's good economic performance over the last decade. However, there are significant foreign investment restrictions in many areas. Country A is also known for providing substantial subsidies to the country's service industry, especially the health and transport sectors. These subsidies have caused much inefficiency. Recently, the government has been faced with growing complaints about the deteriorating standards in health care.

Country A has restrictive laws on the employment of foreign workers, including professionals. As a rule, no foreign professional accreditations are recognized, except the accreditations of a limited number of developed countries. Essentially, all professions are regulated, and citizenship and residency requirements apply in most cases. Furthermore, more restrictive immigration regulations have recently been introduced to address growing security concerns. Customs has been given greater discretionary power to conduct additional security checks at the borders. This has created uncertainty over the amount of time required for trucks to cross Country A's borders and for cargo processing at the ports of entry. While the balance of trade in goods showed a surplus between 2002 and the first half of 2007, the balance in services was in deficit. Country A continues to be a net importer of services.

Trade and foreign investment are particularly important for Country A, which is the world's eighth largest merchandise trader. The trade in goods and services represented the equivalent of close to 70 percent of Country A's GDP in 2007. However, productivity growth has been relatively slow. This has often been compounded by delays in filling vacancies in professional positions. Productivity might be increased by, among other initiatives, removing the restrictions on foreign investment, minimizing subsidies that distort competition, and reforming regulations that impose numerous licensing requirements.

Health service sector—The government of Country A is the main source of funding for health care because it plays a key role in the insurance market. Every citizen of Country A is entitled to insurance and to receive comprehensive health services under the Country A Health Act. Since 2005, the list of services included in the health care insurance plan covered by the government has been reviewed annually. Faced with growing health care costs, the government has removed some nonessential procedures from the list of publicly funded health services (deinsurance).

The private sector plays a significant role. Private health insurance provides additional coverage for health services that are not insured through the public plan. The citizens of Country A also have the option of buying enhanced private plans that provide coverage for nonessential services normally not covered by the government plan (medicines, massages, physiotherapy, and dental services). Furthermore, the government does not deliver publicly insured health services. The delivery of health care in Country A is largely the responsibility of the private sector: most medical practitioners are in private practice, and hospitals are generally private nonprofit organizations. However, the provision of and remuneration for physician and hospital services are subject to government regulation. Laboratory and diagnostic services paid for through public health insurance are delivered by private for-profit facilities.

Most dental services are covered by private insurance plans. The government only provides limited dental care for low-income individuals on social assistance. In recent years, this needs-based dental program has been facing criticism. Because of the huge demand, the wait for treatment in government-run dental clinics can be more than a year. There also concerns about the condition of equipment. There are several reasons for these problems, including chronic underfunding and a shortage in dental health professionals. The government has no additional resources to build and manage more dental clinics to meet the demand. As a result, there are only two publically run dental clinics in the capital (population 3 million), one of the largest cities in Country A. The same clinics are now being used to provide eye examinations and psychotherapy for the poor in cases of medical necessity. The wait for these services, which have recently been deinsured, is about 15 months.

Over the last decade, hospitals have experienced shortages in nursing and other health professionals. The population of the country is rapidly aging. Country A's birth rate has declined. It is estimated that, by the year 2030, approximately 20 percent of Country A's population—one person in five—will be over 65. This demographic transition is exerting pressure on the already overburdened health care system. The system is funded through revenues from the progressive tax structure. However, because of the aging population, the costs associated with health care have increased, and the public health care system is facing growing budgetary problems.

Logistics services—In Country A in the past, logistics were an in-house activity in the manufacturing and distribution sectors. Businesses would respond to their logistics needs by designating staff and resources for the required activities. Increasingly, logistics services are emerging as a separate service sector in which specialized firms offer services on a contract basis. Businesses now rely more on the outsourcing of one or several logistics functions to 3PL service providers.

3PL firms specialize in integrated logistics services. They address the logistics needs of their clients by integrating transport, warehousing, inventory control, order processing, customs brokerage, and other logistics activities in a comprehensive and seamless supply chain management system. They provide logistics services tailored to their clients. Their rapid growth is directly linked to the increasing trend of outsourcing supply chain management activities. Certain industries tend to have recourse to 3PL firms. For example, relative to the automotive, chemical, and retail industries, the high-technology, electronics, and consumer products industries tend to make greater use of 3PL services.

Fourth-party logistics services take the 3PL concept one step further by focusing on the integration of all companies in the supply chain. This guarantees that the planning, management, and monitoring of all logistics procedures are carried out by a single service provider with a long-term strategic objective. A fourth-party logistics service acts as a super manager who supervises all aspects of the supply chain of a manufacturer or distributor and is the sole point of contact between that company and the array of logistics and information service providers (UNCTAD 2006b).

Doing business in Country A is far from perfect. Country A's logistics services are still constrained by regulatory and institutional challenges. Logistics services must deal with a cluster of complex measures that affect various aspects of the processes in which they are involved. Thus, for instance, regulations requiring approvals by several regulatory agencies are cumbersome; they should be streamlined. In Country A, all commercial truck drivers must be members of professional associations and face twice yearly driving tests. Foreign truck drivers are subject to numerous licensing regulations, and the process of obtaining a permit to drive a truck in Country A may take up to six months. There are also new immigration laws and random security checks at the borders. The processing of entry visas for professionals, executives, and authorized service providers is slow and should be accelerated. These few examples illustrate the need for a wide-ranging review of market access and national treatment barriers to trade, but also of regulatory and administrative constraints that keep the cost of doing business high and, hence, impede the production and delivery of many goods and services.

The Country A Security and Customs Act—The articles of the Country A Security and Customs Act provide as follows:

1. The Ministry of Trade may designate customs officers for a specified purpose or, generally, for business relating to customs and immigration and may, at any time, amend, cancel, or reinstate any such designation.

2. The ministry may change the regulations relating to customs and immigration if required. Notice of 48 hours should be given and published on the Country A customs and immigration notice board.
3. Customs officers are to be given special discretionary powers to ensure the security of Country A's borders.
4. Any individual crossing Country A's borders must comply with the most recent regulations. All business people must be able to show all required forms and permits. Failure to present all required documentation may result in delays or refusal of entry.
5. To be a licensed customs broker or establish a brokerage firm in Country A, an individual must be a Country A citizen, or permanent resident, or a corporation. The corporation must be incorporated in Country A, and the majority of the directors must be Country A citizens or permanent residents.
6. The ministry may make regulations prescribing qualifications as to knowledge of the laws and procedures relating to imports and exports and any other qualifications that must be met by an applicant for a customs broker license.

Country B.
Population: 30 million
GDP per capita in 2007: US$5,000
Annual average economic growth in 2004–07: 4 percent

Country B's negotiating team includes government officials, as follows:

• Representative(s) of the Ministry of Trade
• Representative (s) of the Ministry of Transport
• Representative(s) of the Ministry of Health and Welfare
• Representative (s) of the Ministry of Finance

Stakeholders observing the negotiation process include the following:

• Representative(s) of the Country B Business Coalition
• Representative(s) of the Association of Health Care Professionals
• Representative(s) of the Country B Regulatory Transport Commission
• Representative(s) of the Country B Development Association

Relevant economic data—The Country B is a middle-income, landlocked, developing country that shares a border with Country A. Since 1998, the country has been pursuing liberalizing reforms in an effort to reverse previous inward-looking policies. During the last four years, Country B has achieved an average annual growth rate of 4 percent. However, macroeconomic imbalances have again precipitated economic stagnation. The economy has shown large budget deficits, the core of Country B's current economic difficulties. Between 2002 and 2006, fiscal deficits escalated sharply to 15 percent of GDP. Funded mainly by central bank borrowings, the deficits have severely strained public finances and the banking sector. Faced with the looming economic crisis, the government began implementing corrective measures in 2006 that caused the budget deficit to fall to 10 percent in 2007.

In 1996, agricultural production represented 40 percent of GDP and employed over 50 percent of the population. However, in 2006, because of structural changes and the inability of the government to continue to provide agricultural subsidies, agricultural production fell to 25 percent of GDP. By 2007, less than 30 percent of the population was employed full time as farmers. Manufacturing and mining have traditionally accounted for about 20 percent of GDP, but, because of inefficient infrastructure and the high cost of production, many factories have closed, leading to an increase in the number of the unemployed. Overall, these traditional industries have not been creating a sufficient number of jobs. Meanwhile, the service sector is generally underdeveloped.

The current government supports the continuation of economic reform. Foreign investors are reluctant, however, to establish businesses in Country B. The country puts severe restrictions on foreign investors, and the procedures followed by the Country B Land Commission in granting permits lack transparency. In addition, overly complicated procedures, practices, and formalities related to the packaging, processing (including data processing), and transport of goods have deterred investors from establishing a presence in Country B. Consequently, the cost of doing business in Country B is high. The domestic service sector is inadequate, but foreign competition is not permitted.

There are vast undeveloped areas in the mountainous regions of the country. Many streams flow through these areas, and some of them are known to be rich in minerals and salts. The rich flora includes an abundance of plants with soothing, healing, or medicinal qualities. In short, there is great potential for health tourism. The mountainous regions of the country would be attractive to tourists interested in taking holidays at spas close to warm streams and hot springs. The Country B is a large country with abundant natural resources and mineral-bearing waters.

Health service sector—The government of the Country B is barely coping with the rising cost of health care. The government provides basic health care for all low-income citizens and provides health insurance automatically for all citizens. However, the treatment available through the insurance is basic and mostly covers only individuals under life-threatening circumstances. Moreover, no regulations specifically define the nature of the essential health services that are covered by the public insurance system. As a result, the government has been arbitrarily removing procedures from insurance coverage. Private insurance is also available, but there are only two major providers. Some hospitals are run by the government and employ physicians and nurses paid by the government. Private hospitals and clinics are allowed. No regulations specify the relationship between the government-run system and the private sector financing and delivery of health care. The health care sector is completely closed to foreign competition.

The health sector suffers because of a poor reputation. The government-run hospitals and clinics consume up to 25 percent of the government health budget, but the standards are low. Private hospitals and clinics run notoriously huge budget deficits that allow them to qualify for government subsidies. The sustained subsidies going to the private sector mean that there are no incentives to make health care more efficient. It has recently been reported in the media that a significant share of health care costs are accounted for by administration, including the large health bureaucracy.

Hospitals and clinics are poorly equipped, and public and private insurance schemes are poorly managed. Data management is poor. Thus, for example, the processing of claims takes months because so many forms must be submitted. Because the regulations on health insurance lack precise definitions of the procedures and activities covered, bureaucrats are inconsistent in responding to claims, especially in cases involving multiple procedures. Because the burden of proof rests with the hospitals and clinics, the costs of submitting additional documentation and the time devoted to seeking reimbursements are excessive at every health care facility in the country.

The health care history of patients is not readily available because there is no medical data processing and storage system. Individuals moving from one area of the country to another are responsible for obtaining and transferring their medical files to their new doctors. The fee for this sort of service is prohibitive, and few people maintain their own medical files. Health professionals therefore often have only limited knowledge of the medical history of their patients. New diagnoses are expensive and not regularly carried out. This leads to errors in treatment and waste in the use of resources.

Logistics services—The Country B has the potential to be a competitive exporter of lumber, minerals, and some agricultural products. It could also become an attractive manufacturing base given its productive capacities. However, domestic and foreign companies operating in Country B are unable to bring goods to foreign markets at the lowest possible cost and under the conditions required by customers. Logistics services in Country B are virtually nonexistent. There are no logistics service suppliers in Country B, and the country has yet to liberalize the relevant service sectors, especially transport.

The problem is caused by the limitations on market access and national treatment, including limits on foreign equity capital participation and limitations on establishment, for example, the requirement to form joint ventures with domestic suppliers. Moreover, there are also regulatory constraints, including cumbersome, discriminatory, nontransparent, and nonuniform customs procedures. Inadequate Internet and other digital and electronic infrastructure is aggravated by the shortage in professionals skilled in digital technologies, resulting in poor data collection and storage and unnecessary administrative delays because of the inability to submit documentation electronically.

Reliance only on traditional transport services is insufficient for meeting the needs of today's markets. More efficient and wide-ranging logistics services must be developed that are also proficient in the use of information and communication technologies. Multimodal transport operations involving a single service provider that assumes responsibility for the entire transport chain must be fostered.

Thus, for example, business services are important in the development of modern logistics services. The following services may be especially crucial:

- Professional services (legal, accounting, bookkeeping)
- Computer and related services
- Research and development services
- Rental and leasing services
- Other business services, including advertising, market research and opinion polling, management consulting, technical testing and analysis, agricultural services, mining services, manufacturing services, printing

and publishing, photography, packaging, convention services, translation and interpretation, design, and data processing.

The Country B Transportation Corporation Act—The articles of the Country B Transportation Corporation Act provide as follows:

1. The government of Country B shall control 60 percent of the common shares of the corporation.
2. The remaining 40 percent of the common shares may be traded on the Country B stock exchange.
3. The Transportation Corporation of Country B shall provide air, road, and rail services in Country B without any additional licensing and permit requirements.
4. The board of directors may annually issue a limited number of permits to private transport companies based on economic needs tests.
5. The Transportation Corporation of Country B shall own all railway stations servicing the rail lines used by the Corporation.
6. The Transportation Corporation of Country B shall own all airports in Country B.
7. All employees of the Transportation Corporation of Country B must be citizens of Country B.
8. The owners of firms that are contracted by the Transportation Corporation of Country B for the purpose of improving operations (for example, providers of business services) must be citizens of Country B.

Country C.
Population: 120 million
GDP per capita in 2007: US$18,000
Annual average economic growth in 2004–07: 5 percent

Country C's negotiating team includes government officials, as follows:

- Representative(s) of the Ministry of Trade
- Representative (s) of the Ministry of Transport
- Representative(s) of the Ministry of Health and Welfare
- Representative (s) of the Ministry of Finance

Stakeholders observing the negotiation process include the following:

- Representative(s) of the Tourist Association of Country C
- Representative(s) of the Bureau of Public Roads of Country C

- Representative(s) of the Bureau of Professional Accreditations
- Representative(s) of the Country C Manufacturing Business Alliance

Relevant economic data—Since it started the process of transformation from an interventionist to an open economy model two decades ago, Country C has become more outward oriented. The ongoing structural reforms, including liberalization of the trade and investment regimes, have contributed to stable economic expansion. Growth has averaged 5 percent annually, much of this attributable to exports. The trade in goods and services increased from 89 percent of GDP in 2004 to approximately 90 percent in 2007. Nonetheless, the maintenance of government ownership in transport services and of conflicting regulations on the professions and on overall investment has hindered competition and promoted high logistics costs and low labor productivity in many areas of the economy.

Inward foreign direct investment declined from 1.5 percent of GDP in 2004 to 0.5 percent in 2007. This is considered low by the standards of developed countries. The decline and low level of inward foreign direct investment in relation to GDP can be attributed to the increasing cost of doing business in Country C, the country's often-baffling regulations, and the existing restrictions. Despite the introduction of a more open foreign investment regime, several sectors remain completely closed to foreign investors, and many are partially restricted. The service sector is characterized by low labor productivity and declining growth; this is because of insufficient competition as a result of unduly burdensome regulations, the predominance of state-owned enterprises, and low foreign presence. Customs procedures have not yet been streamlined and modernized. Foreign direct investment in Country C is subject to the Country C Investment Act.

Health service sector—A two-tier public-private system, the health service sector in Country C is inefficient, encumbered with conflicting regulations, and overburdened. Public health insurance is needs based. Private health insurance is supplied through one provider. The public is critical of the sector as are surgeons, emergency response experts, and others especially frustrated because of the poor quality of trauma services in Country C. For instance, in the capital of Country C, there are only 35 public ambulances with emergency life-saving equipment available to serve a population of 12 million. The health care system is inequitable, despite the country's recent economic growth. Still, more and more foreigners have been coming to Country C for heart surgeries or hip replacements in private hospitals that offer single rooms and butler services. Meanwhile, public hospitals are sometimes so overcrowded that patients are obliged to share beds. Many are forced to ask relatives for money so that they may transfer to private hospitals with computed tomography scanners or dialysis machines. Country C spends 1 percent of GDP on public health, far less than other countries at similar levels of per capita income. While the cost of private clinics and hospitals is out of the reach of most citizens of Country C, the public sector system suffers from inadequate funding.

The public sector is divided into A1 and A2 providers of health services. A1 hospitals and clinics serve only government officials and members of the military. A2 hospitals and clinics serve low-income groups. Over the years, this division has been heavily criticized. It is well documented that the health care standards in the A1 facilities are much higher because A1 providers receive most of the government health care funding.

Country C has well-developed business services especially in the field of data storage. The technology sector is, in fact, a success story in Country C. This is why policy makers should promote the export of services, such as data entry of health records and of health insurance claims, as a way to generate income and employment in the country. (Under the GATS, health data processing and storage services are not classified under health services, but under computer-related services.)

Logistics services—Services that contribute to enhancing the competitiveness of production processes and delivery—the supply chain—are known as logistics services. Logistics services are crucial for achieving and maintaining a higher level of development.

Businesses operating in Country C complain about logistics and transport delays. There are many challenges that the government of Country C must address, in consultation with private stakeholders. The complexities of logistics services mean that the government must examine its interests in market access and the regulatory, infrastructural, and institutional constraints in the country.

An example of an area in which immediate improvements may be made is exports. Given that Country C moves most of its exports and receives its imports by sea, the efficient processing of cargos at the country's four main harbors is critical. However, cargo containers are often lost or burglarized. Because of the administrative delays and poor communications between truck drivers and harbor officials, cargo containers are routinely kept outside within the harbor area for up to two days before drivers are able to haul them away. There is no secured storage or warehouse facilities. Even companies that hire security firms to guard their containers are unable to guarantee the contents from loss or theft.

The Country C Investment Act—The articles of the Country C Investment Act provide as follows:

1. The Ministry of Investment shall carry out market analysis on domestic and international investment. The ministry shall have authority to determine the scope of economic needs tests that relate to foreign investment initiatives and of work permits for foreign workers and professionals. The ministry's determination will be made in accordance with the following: (a) the effect of the investments on the level and nature of economic activity in Country C, including employment and the use of parts, components, and services produced in Country C, and (b) the scope of participation by citizens of Country C in the proposed investments.
2. The act applies to foreign investments through acquisitions, mergers, and takeovers, as well as new investments and portfolio investments. The minimum capital necessary for foreign investments is US$100,000 in the case of joint ventures and US$400,000 for projects wholly owned by foreigners. All investments by non-citizens of Country C exceeding US$500,000 are subject to an application process that must be reviewed by the ministry. An applicant shall receive a reply within 12 months of the submission of the application.
3. The act reserves certain business activities to citizens of Country C. These are the top management positions in businesses with more than 50 employees, all insurance agents, and supervisors on public construction projects. The Ministry of Investment may make exceptions to this rule based on economic needs tests.
4. The ministry may impose requirements or enforce any commitment or undertaking in connection with the location of production, the employment and training of workers, and the construction or expansion of individual facilities in Country C.
5. The ministry may designate immigration officers solely responsible for issuing special business visas and related permits. Country C has specific visa requirements. Only top executives of foreign companies may obtain automatic three-month renewable visas. All other foreigners, including professionals, must apply for special visa permits issued by the Ministry of Investment or the Ministry of Trade. The application process should not exceed three months.

Instructions for Conducting the Second Part of the Exercise
The second part of the negotiation exercise covers the actual negotiations and the preparation of revised schedules and final reports.

The aim of the second part of the exercise. The delegations representing Countries A, B, and C must negotiate with their trading partners to fulfill the priorities they have each identified.

Concluding the second, final part of the exercise. To conclude the second part of the exercise, each of the three negotiating teams must prepare the following documents:

1. New, revised, and improved schedules of specific commitments
2. Two brief report notes: one by the private stakeholders, and one by the government representatives

To prepare the documents, each country team is expected to do the following:

- Consult with private stakeholders.
- Engage in the negotiation process.
- Work as a team, but with a designated chairperson.
- Consult with private stakeholders as the negotiations unfold.
- Conclude the negotiations to the best of the team's abilities.
- Prepare the revised schedule of commitments.
- The private stakeholders should prepare a brief note assessing the process and the outcome of the negotiations from the point of view of private stakeholders.
- The government team should prepare a brief note assessing the process and the outcome of the negotiations from the point of view of the government.

The instructor who conducts the exercise will hold an open evaluation session to share comments on the process and the outcome of the exercise.

Annex 4A   Health-Related Services

Table 4A.1.   Health-Related Services: Relevant Sectors and the Corresponding CPC Classifications

WTO sectoral classification list	CPC code	CPC definition
1. Business services		
A. Professional services		
(h) Medical and dental services	CPC 9312	*General medical services:* services consisting of the prevention, diagnosis, and treatment by medical doctors of physical or mental diseases of a general nature —consultations —physical checkups, and so on. These services are not limited to specified or particular conditions, diseases, or anatomical regions. They may be provided in the practices of general practitioners and also delivered by outpatient clinics, clinics attached to firms, schools, and so on. *Specialized medical services* *Includes:* —consultation services in pediatrics, gynecology-obstetrics, neurology and psychiatry, and various medical services —surgical consultation services —treatment services in outpatient clinics, such as dialysis, chemotherapy, insulin therapy, respirator treatment, X-ray treatment, and the like —functional exploration and interpretation of medical images (X-ray photographs, electrocardiograms, endoscopies, and the like) *Does not include:* —services of medical laboratories, for example, 93199 *Dental services* —orthodontic services, for example, treatment of protruding teeth, cross bite, overbite, and so on, including dental surgery for inpatients in hospitals

(continued)

Table 4A.1. Health-Related Services: Relevant Sectors and the Corresponding CPC Classifications *(continued)*

WTO sectoral classification list	CPC code	CPC definition
		—services in oral surgery
		—other specialized dental services, for example, in periodontics, pedodontics, endodontics, and reconstruction
		—diagnosis and treatment services for diseases affecting the patient or aberrations in the cavity of the mouth and services aimed at the prevention of dental diseases
(i) Veterinary services	CPC 932	*Veterinary services for pet animals (93210)*
		—animal and veterinary hospital and nonhospital medical, surgical, and dental services delivered to pet animals. The services are aimed at curing, restoring, or maintaining the health of the animal.
		—hospital, laboratory, and technical services, foods (including special diets), and other facilities and resources
		Veterinary services for livestock (93220)
		—animal and veterinary hospital and nonhospital medical, surgical, and dental services delivered to livestock. The services are aimed at curing, restoring, or maintaining the health of the animal.
		—hospital, laboratory, and technical services, foods (including special diets), and other facilities and resources
		Other veterinary services (93290)
		—animal and veterinary hospital and nonhospital medical, surgical, and dental services delivered to animals other than pets or livestock (including zoo animals and animals raised for fur production or other products). The services are aimed at curing, restoring, or maintaining the health of the animal.
		—hospital, laboratory, and technical services, foods (including special diets), and other facilities and resources

(j) Services provided by midwives, nurses, physiotherapists, and paramedical personnel

CPC 93191

—services such as supervision during pregnancy and childbirth
—supervision of the mother after birth
—services in nursing care (without admission), advice and prevention for patients at home, the provision of maternity care, children's hygiene, and so on
—services provided by physiotherapists and other paramedical persons (including homeopathic and similar services)
—physiotherapy and paramedical services are services in the field of physiotherapy, ergotherapy, occupational therapy, speech therapy, homeopathy, acupuncture, nutrition, and so on; these services are provided by authorized persons other than medical doctors

7. Financial services
A. All insurance and insurance-related services

(a) Life, accident, and health insurance services

CPC 8121

Accident and health insurance services
—underwriting services of insurance policies that provide protection for hospital and medical expenses not covered by government programs and usually other health care expenses such as prescribed drugs, medical appliances, ambulance, private duty nursing, and so on
—underwriting services of insurance policies that provide protection for dental expenses
—underwriting services of insurance policies that provide protection for medical expenses incurred in traveling outside a certain geographical area
—underwriting services of insurance policies that provide periodic payments if the insured individual is unable to work as a result of a disability due to illness or injury
—underwriting services of insurance policies that provide accidental death and dismemberment insurance, that is, payment in the event that an accident results in death or loss of one or more bodily parts (such as hands or feet) or the sight of one or both eyes

(continued)

Table 4A.1. Health-Related Services: Relevant Sectors and the Corresponding CPC Classifications *(continued)*

WTO sectoral classification list	CPC code	CPC definition
8. Health-related and social services		
A. Hospital services	CPC 9311	—surgical services delivered under the direction of medical doctors chiefly to inpatients and aimed at curing, restoring, or maintaining the health of patients
		—medical services delivered under the direction of medical doctors chiefly to inpatients and aimed at curing, restoring, or maintaining the health of patients
		—gynecological and obstetrical services delivered under the direction of medical doctors chiefly to inpatients and aimed at curing, restoring, or maintaining the health of patients
		—rehabilitation services delivered under the direction of medical doctors chiefly to inpatients and aimed at curing, restoring, or maintaining the health of patients
		—psychiatric services delivered under the direction of medical doctors chiefly to inpatients and aimed at curing, restoring, or maintaining the health of patients
		—other hospital services delivered under the direction of medical doctors chiefly to inpatients and aimed at curing, restoring, or maintaining the health of patients; these services comprise medical, pharmaceutical, and paramedical services; nursing services; laboratory and technical services, including radiological and anesthesiological services; and so on
		—military hospital services
		—prison hospital services
B. Other human health services	CPC 9319 (other than 93191)	*Ambulance services*
		—services involving the transport of patients by ambulance, with or without resuscitation equipment or medical personnel
		Residential health facility services other than hospital services
		—combined lodging and medical services provided without the supervision of a medical doctor located on the premises

Other human health services

—services provided by medical laboratories

—services provided by blood, sperm, and transplant organ banks

—dental testing services

—medical analysis and testing services

—other human health services not elsewhere classified

C. Social services   CPC 933   *Welfare services delivered through residential institutions to elderly persons and persons with disabilities*

Includes:

—social assistance services involving round-the-clock care at residential institutions for elderly persons

—social assistance services involving round-the-clock care at residential institutions for persons with physical or intellectual disabilities, including those having disabilities in seeing, hearing, or speaking

Does not include:

—education services, for instance, 92

—combined lodging and medical services, for example, 93110 (hospital services), if under the direction of medical doctors, and 93193, if without supervision by a medical doctor

Other social services with accommodation

—residential social assistance services involving round-the-clock care for children, for example, social services for orphanages, homes for children in need of protection, homes for children with emotional impairments

—residential social assistance services involving round-the-clock care for other clients, for example, homes for single mothers, juvenile correction homes

—rehabilitation services (not including medical treatment) for persons with impairments such as alcohol or drug dependence

—other social rehabilitation services

Sources: WTO 1991; UN 1991.

Notes

1. A commitment is a legally binding undertaking specific to a country under one of the agreements administered by the WTO (Goode 2007).
2. This section is based on Cattaneo (2010).
3. The Millennium Development Goals pertaining to health include goal 4 (reduce by two-thirds the mortality rate among children under 5), goal 5 (reduce by three-quarters the maternal mortality ratio; achieve, by 2015, universal access to reproductive health), and goal 6 (halt and begin to reverse the spread of HIV/AIDS; achieve, by 2010, universal access to treatment for HIV/AIDS for all those who need it; halt and begin to reverse the incidence of malaria and other major diseases).
4. This subsection is based on Blouin, Drager, and Smith (2006).
5. Documents accompanying this exercise are provided at http://go.world bank.org/DLM9JWE9A0. Users will find suggested instructions for each country, as well as the relevant schedule of commitments that will allow users to complete the information required to carry out the exercise.
6. The descriptions provided of countries A, B, and C do not represent any existing country. Participants are encouraged to use fictitious names for their countries during the exercise.
7. Such a schedule may be found at http://go.worldbank.org/DLM9JWE9A0.

References

Arvis, Jean-François, Monica Alina Mustra, Lauri Ojala, Ben Shepherd, and Daniel Saslavsky. 2010. "Connecting to Compete 2010: Trade Logistics in the Global Economy; The Logistics Performance Index and Its Indicators." Report, World Bank, Washington, DC.

Arvis, Jean-François, Monica Alina Mustra, John Panzer, Lauri Ojala, and Tapio Naula. 2007. "Connecting to Compete: Trade Logistics in the Global Economy; The Logistics Performance Index and Its Indicators." Report, World Bank, Washington, DC.

Blouin, Chantal, Nick Drager, and Richard Smith, eds. 2006. *International Trade in Health Services and the GATS: Current Issues and Debates*. Washington, DC: World Bank.

Cattaneo, Olivier. 2010. "Health without Borders: International Trade for Better Health Systems and Services." In *International Trade in Services: New Trends and Opportunities for Developing Countries*, Olivier Cattaneo, Michael Engman, Sebastián Sáez, and Robert M. Stern, ed. Washington, DC: World Bank.

Deloitte. 2008. "Medical Tourism: Consumers in Search of Value." Deloitte Center for Health Solutions, Washington, DC.

de Souza, Robert, Mark Goh, Sumeet Gupta, and Luo Lei. 2007. "An investigation into the Measures Affecting the Integration of ASEAN's Priority Sectors (Phase 2): The Case of Logistics." REPSF Project 06/001d, Report, Regional Economic Policy Support Facility, Association of Southeast Asian Nations, Manila.

Ghoneim, Ahmed F., and Omneia A. Helmy. 2007. "Maritime Transport and Related Logistics Services in Egypt." Issue Paper 8 (December), Programme on Trade in Services and Sustainable Development, International Centre for Trade and Sustainable Development, Geneva.

Goode, Walter. 2007. *Dictionary of Trade Policy Terms*. 5th ed. New York: Cambridge University Press.

Hoekman, Bernard, and Alessandro Nicita. 2008. "Trade Policy, Trade Costs, and Developing Country Trade." Policy Research Working Paper 4797, World Bank, Washington, DC.

Hollweg, Claire, and Marn-Heong Wong. 2009. "Measuring Regulatory Restrictions in Logistics Services." ERIA Discussion Paper d017 (May), Economic Research Institute for ASEAN and East Asia, Jakarta.

HP Enterprise Services. 2009. "Government Supply Chain: Synchronization, Speed, and Security in Government Logistics." *Government Journal* 1 (3), HP Enterprise Services, Plano, TX. http://h10134.www1.hp.com/industries/gov ernment/journal/.

McLinden, G., E. Fanta, D. Widdowson, and T. Doyle. 2010. *Border Management Modernization: A Practical Guide for Reformers*. Washington, DC: World Bank.

Memedovic, Olga, Lauri Ojala, Jean-Paul Rodrigue, and Tapio Naula. 2008. "Fuelling the Global Value Chains: What Role for Logistics Capabilities?" *International Journal of Technological Learning, Innovation and Development* 1 (3): 353–74.

Portugal-Perez, Alberto, and John S. Wilson. 2008. "Why Trade Facilitation Matters to Africa." Policy Research Working Paper 4719, World Bank, Washington, DC.

UN (United Nations). 1991. "Provisional Central Product Classification (Provisional CPC)." Document ST/ESA/STAT/SER.M/77, Economic Statistics and Classifications Section, Statistics Division, Department of Economic and Social Affairs, United Nations, New York. http://unstats.un.org/unsd/class/family/family2.asp?Cl=9.

UNCTAD (United Nations Conference on Trade and Development). 2006a. "Negotiations on Transport and Logistics Services: Issues to Consider." Report UNCTAD/SDTE/TLB/2005/3, UNCTAD, Geneva.

———. 2006b. "Trade and Development Aspects of Logistics Services: Note by the UNCTAD Secretariat." Document TD/B/COM.1/AHM.1/2 (July 7), Trade and Development Board, UNCTAD, Geneva.

USITC (United States International Trade Commission). 2004. *Express Delivery Services: Competitive Conditions Facing U.S.–Based Firms in Foreign Markets.* Publication 3678, Investigation 332–456. Washington, DC: USITC.

———. 2005. *Logistic Services: An Overview of the Global Market and Potential Effects of Removing Trade Impediments.* Publication 3770, Investigation 332–463. Washington, DC: USITC.

World Bank. 2006. "Infraestructura logística y de calidad para la competitividad de Colombia." Report 35061-CO, Sustainable Development Department, Latin America and the Caribbean Region, World Bank, Washington, DC.

———. 2007. "Port Reform Toolkit." World Bank, Washington, DC. http://go.worldbank.org/1CN4CR6GH0.

———. 2009. "Uruguay Trade and Logistics: An Opportunity." Unpublished report, September 30, World Bank, Washington, DC.

WTO (World Trade Organization). 1991. "Services Sectoral Classification List: Note by the Secretariat." Document MTN.GNS/W/120 (July 10), WTO, Geneva.

———. 1993. "General Agreement on Trade in Services." WTO, Geneva. http://www.wto.org/english/docs_e/legal_e/26-gats.pdf.

———. 2004. "Communication from Australia; Hong Kong, China; Liechtenstein; Mauritius; New Zealand; Nicaragua; Switzerland, and the Separate Customs Territory of Taiwan, Penghu, Kinmen, and Matsu: Logistics Services." Document TN/S/W/20 (June 25), Council for Trade in Services, WTO, Geneva.

Index

Boxes, figures, notes, and tables are indicated by *b, f, n,* and *t,* respectively.

A

A. T. Kearney, 13
adjustment pressures, 80–81
Africa. *See also* Sub-Saharan Africa, and
    specific countries
    Middle East and North Africa,
        diversification of exports, 2
aid for trade in services, 14, 21, 76–81
    adjustment pressures, 80–81
    agenda for, devising, 81
    EPAs, 5, 77, 78–80*b*
    regulatory capacity-building,
        58–61, 59–61*b*
    tariffs, 80
    trade-related technical assistance,
        61–62, 62–63*b*
Arab Republic of Egypt, 129
Argentina, 124
ASEAN (Association of Southeast Asian
    Nations), 121
Asia. *See also* specific countries
    ASEAN, 121
    diversification of exports through
        services in, 2
    East Asia and Pacific, agreements with
        European Union in, 5
Economic and Social Commission for
    Asia and the Pacific, 82*n*2
Europe and Central Asia, openness of
    regime in, 8
Asian Development Bank, 82*n*2
Association of Southeast Asian Nations
    (ASEAN), 121
audits, trade-related regulatory, 36–42,
    37–40*b*, 42–42*b*

B

Bangladesh, 124
Bank for International Settlements, 38
Botswana, 124
Brazil, 2, 124

C

Canada, 12, 40*b*, 73–74*b*
capacity to supply. *See* supply capacity,
    enhancing
CARICOM, 5, 87–88
CARIFORUM, 5, 77, 78–80*b*,
    83*n*12, 87–88
Centre for the Promotion of Imports
    in the Netherlands, 73

Chile, 2, 13, 111*b*, 124
China, 59–60*b*, 83*n*8, 124
Coalition of Service Industries, 70*b*
commitments
    defined, 168*n*1
    modes of supply, sorting by, 109
    SERET. *See under* service regulations
        management tool
    under GATS, 93*t*, 94–95, 94*t*
conducting negotiations, 21, 44–53
    Doha Round shift toward collective
        requests, 46, 47–48*b*, 52
    factors in formulating request or offer,
        49, 50–51*f*
    market opening, 46–53, 80–81, 81–82*n*1
    negotiation exercise (Part 2), 162
    pertinent concerns, 54–55*b*
    rule making process, 45–46
Congo, Democratic Republic of, 124
coordination of stakeholders, 27–35,
        28–30*b*, 31–33*t*, 34*f*, 35*f*, 82*n*4
Costa Rica, 2, 134
Cotonou Agreement, 78*b*
Council for Trade in Services, 91
CPC (United Nations Provisional
        Central Product Classification),
        131, 163–167*t*
Croatia, 124
crossborder trade
    as mode of supply, 7, 12
    health services, 138, 142
    negotiating, 30, 46, 75
    relative success at, 13
    SERET and, 91, 98–99, 103, 109
cultural exceptions to international
        agreements, 12

D

database for trade in services
        management. *See* service
        regulations management tool
de Souza, Robert, 130
Deardoff, Alan V., 8–9
Deloitte Consulting, 134
Democratic Republic of Congo, 124
deregulation. *See* liberalization of
        trade in services
development. *See* strategic development
        role of trade in services
differential and special treatment of
        developing countries, 14

discriminatory and nondiscriminatory
        regulations, 8–9, 9*t*, 89–91,
        90*t*, 91*t*
Doha Round
    collective requests, shift toward, 46,
        47–48*b*, 52
    Doha Development Agenda, 20, 77
    impact of nonservice trade negotiations
        on service negotiations, 53
    logistics services negotiations, 125
Dominican Republic, 5, 88

E

East Asia and Pacific, agreements with
        European Union in, 5. *See also*
        specific countries
Economic and Social Commission for Asia
        and the Pacific, 82*n*2
Economic Partnership Agreements (EPAs),
        5, 77, 78–80*b*
economy-wide implications of
        service-sector reform, 22–23
Egypt, Arab Republic of, 129
entry and establishment, regulations
        affecting, 8–9, 9*t*
EPAs (Economic Partnership Agreements),
        5, 77, 78–80*b*
Eritrea, 124
Europe and Central Asia, openness of
        regime in, 8. *See also* specific
        countries
European Commission, 82*n*2, 83*n*12
European Union
    all trade agreements with now involving
        trade in services, 5, 87–88
    CARIFORUM and CARICOM
        agreements, 5, 77, 78–80*b*,
        83*n*12, 87–88
    exceptions, negotiating, 12
    GATS, use of, 6, 121
    liberalization model, 97
    Treaty of Rome (1958), 115–116*n*3
European Union–China Trade Project,
        59–60*b*
exceptions, negotiating, 12

F

Feketekuty, Geza, 20
Fiji, 124
Francois, Joseph E., 7
freight logistics. *See* logistics services

G

Gabon, 124
General Agreement on Tariffs and Trade
     (GATT), 81, 92–94, 94t
General Agreement on Trade in
     Services (GATS)
  capacity-building efforts tending to
     focus on, 25–26
  commitments under, 93t, 94–95, 94t
  conducting negotiations, 46, 48
  GATT compared, 81, 92–94, 94t
  health services, 141, 142–143
  importance of, 6
  International Trade Centre consultation
     kit, 82n3
  liberalization and, 80, 95–96,
     97, 99, 112
  logistics services, 130–134
  market access restrictions, 93–94, 93t
  multilateral framework, 91–94, 92–94t
  negotiation exercise, as framework
     for, 121
  regulatory weaknesses, addressing, 56
  stakeholders, coordination of, 28
  supply capacity, enhancing, 73
  trade-related regulatory audits, 39
  Uruguay Round, broader obligations
     emerging from, 53
Ghani, Eja, 3
Ghoneim, Ahmed F, 129
Gootiiz, Batshur, 13
government, coordination within,
     27–30, 28–30b, 35f
Greece, 124

H

health services, 134–147
  crossborder trade, 138, 142
  development of negotiating positions,
     issues to consider for, 142–143,
     144–146t
  GATS and, 141, 142–143
  in negotiation exercise, 122
     country A, description of, 151–152
     country B, description of, 156–157
     country C, description of, 159–160
  modes of supply, 138, 139t, 142
  potential benefits and drawbacks,
     138, 142
  regulatory issues, 140, 142–143
  supply and demand, 134–138

Helmy, Omneia A., 129
Hoekman, Bernard, xii, 7
human capital
  importance of, 13–14
  training. See training

I

implementing negotiated outcomes,
     21, 53–55, 64b
India, 2, 13, 83n8, 124, 134
Indonesia Trade Assistance, 60–61b
information access issues, 82–83n6, 88.
     See also service regulations
     management tool
infrastructure, restrictions on access and
     use of, 126–129, 127–128t
Inter-American Development Bank, 82n2
intergovernmental coordination, 27–30,
     28–30b, 35f
international agreements, strategic
     development role of, 11–14
International Association of Insurance
     Supervisors, 38
International Chamber of Commerce, 71b
International Organization of Securities
     Commissions, 38
International Trade Centre, 72b, 82n2

J

Japan, 5, 87
Japan-Philippines Economic Partnership
     Agreement, 41b

K

Kenya, 2

L

Lanoszka, Anna, 121
Latin America and Caribbean. See also
     specific countries
  crossborder supply in, 13
  diversification of exports through
     services in, 2
  European Union, agreements with,
     5, 78–80b, 83n12, 87–88
  logistics services in, 124
  openness of regime in, 8
liberalization of trade in services
  assessment of impact, 9–10
  defined, 7

European Union model of, 97
GATS and, 80, 95–96, 97, 99, 112
importance of, 3
NAFTA model, 97–99, 109–110, 112
openness/protectiveness of regimes
  measuring, 7–8
  performance and, 13
progressive liberalization, 77
PTAs, through, 95–101, 100t
reform strategy, designing, 10–11
regulation and, 7, 8–9, 56
strategic nature of, 6–11
Libya, 140
logistics services, 123–134
  core freight logistics, 125–126,
    131, 132–133t
  defined, 123
  foreign trade management constraints,
    127–128t, 130
  in GATS, 130–134
  in negotiation exercise, 122
    country A, description of, 152–153
    country B, description of, 157–158
    country C, description of, 160–161
  increasing tradability of, 2–3
  noncore freight logistics, 126,
    132–133t, 132–134
  overperformers and
    underperformers, 124t
  regulatory issues, 125–126,
    127–128t, 130
  related freight logistics, 126,
    131, 132–133t
  restrictions on trade in, 126–130,
    127–128t
  special issues involved in development
    of negotiating position on,
    134, 135–137t
  WTO negotiation proposal,
    131, 132–133t

M

Madagascar, 124
Marconini, Mario, 19
market access restrictions, 93–94,
  93t, 126, 127–128t
market opening, 46–53, 80–81, 81–82n1
Mattoo, Aaditya, 13, 81
medical tourism. See health services
Mercosur or Southern Common
  Market, 121, 124

Mexico
  crossborder supply in, 13
  diversification of exports through
    services in, 2
  European Union, trade agreement
    with, 5, 87
  exceptions, negotiating, 12
  trade-related regulatory audits, 41–42b
Middle East and North Africa,
  diversification of exports in, 2.
  See also specific countries
Millennium Development Goals,
  138, 168n3
modes of supply
  GATS classification of, 91–92, 92t
  health services, 138, 139t, 142
  negotiating, 12, 74–75
Montenegro, 124
Morocco, 2
most favored nation clauses, 89, 92

N

NAFTA. See North American Free Trade
  Agreement
Namibia, 124
national development strategy
  negotiation process, importance
    to, 26–27
  policy making and reform
    for, 22–24, 24–25b
negotiation exercise, 121–170
  as part of broader course
    work, 147–148
  conducting negotiation (Part 2), 162
  country A, description of, 150–154
  country B, description of, 154–158
  country C, description of, 158–161
  GATS as framework for, 121
  goals and objectives, 122–123, 147–148
  health services in, 122. See also
    health services
  length of simulation, 147
  logistics services in, 122. See also
    logistics services
  number of participants, 147
  preparation of negotiating position
    (Part 1), 148–149
negotiation of agreements, 4–5, 19–68
  aid for. See aid for trade in services
  conducting. See conducting negotiations
  exceptions, 12

implementing negotiated outcomes,
    21, 53–55, 64*b*
mapping strategy for, 21–24, 24–25*b*
modes of supply, 12, 74–75
nonservice negotiations, impact of, 53
preparation for. *See* preparation for
    negotiation of agreements
regulatory weaknesses, addressing,
    55–63, 59–61*b*
strategic nature of, 12–13
supply capacity. *See* supply capacity,
    enhancing
nonservice trade negotiations, impact
    of, 53
nondiscriminatory and discriminatory
    regulations, 8–9, 9*t*, 89–91,
    90*t*, 91*t*
North American Free Trade Agreement
    (NAFTA)
    exceptions, 12
    liberalization model, 97–99,
        109–110, 112
    trade-related regulatory audits, 39*b*,
        40*b*, 41–42*b*

O

operations, regulations affecting, 8–9, 9*t*
Organisation for Economic Co-operation
    and Development (OECD), 8,
    63, 73, 74
Organization of American States
    (OAS), 82*n*2

P

Paraguay, 124
Philippines, 2, 41*b*, 124, 129
policy making and reform, 4
    as national development strategy,
        22–24, 24–25*b*
    coordination of stakeholders in, 33, 34*f*
    service coalitions, 70–71*b*
preferential trade agreements (PTAs)
    classification, ordered by year of
        notification to WTO, 98, 113–115*t*
    conducting negotiations, 45
    liberalization through, 95–101, 100*t*
    preparation for negotiations, 28, 36, 40*b*
    regulatory weaknesses, addressing, 55, 56
    segmentation of management of, 83*n*8
    success of unilateral efforts *versus*, 20
    supply capacity, enhancing, 73, 77

preparation for negotiation of agreements,
    21, 25–42
    coordination of stakeholders, 27–35,
        28–30*b*, 31–33*t*, 34*f*, 35*f*, 82*n*4
    key questions arising during, 43–44*b*
    national development strategy,
        establishing, 26–27
    negotiation exercise (Part 1), 148–149
    trade-related regulatory audits, 36–42,
        37–40*b*, 42–42*b*
PTAs. *See* preferential trade agreements

R

regulatory issues, 4
    analytical structure of, 8–9, 9*t*
    discriminatory and nondiscriminatory
        regulation, 8–9, 9*t*, 89–91, 90*t*, 91*t*
    health services, 140, 142–143
    in country A, negotiation
        exercise, 153–154
    in country B, negotiation exercise, 158
    in country C, negotiation exercise, 161
    liberalization and regulation, 7, 8–9, 56
    logistics services, 125–126, 127–128*t*, 130
    negotiations as means of addressing
        weaknesses in, 55–63, 59–61*b*
    objectives and instruments of regulation,
        88–89, 90*t*
    SERET. *See* service regulations
        management tool
    supply capacity, enhancing, 73, 75
    trade-related regulatory audits, 36–42,
        37–40*b*, 42–42*b*
Rome, Treaty of (1958), 115–116*n*3
rule making process, 45–46
Russian Federation, 124

S

Sáez, Sebastián, 1, 87, 121
Sauvé, Pierre, 19
sequencing issues, 4–5
SERET. *See* service regulations
    management tool
service coalitions, 69–72*b*
service regulations management tool
    (SERET), 5, 87–119
    classification codes, 104–105, 106*t*
    classification of sectors in, 88, 89*b*
    commitments, 94–95
        GATS commitment schedules,
            93–94, 93*t*

nesting horizontal commitments,
    105, 107–108*t*
positive list commitment schedules,
    103–104, 104*t*
sorting by mode of supply, 109
template, pasting onto, 109
data sources, 101–103, 102*t*
discriminatory and nondiscriminatory
    regulations, 8–9, 9*t*, 89–91, 90*t*, 91*t*
multilateral framework, 91–94, 92–94*t*
negative list approach, 109–112, 111*b*
objectives and instruments of
    regulation, 88–89, 90*t*
positive list approach, 101–109
PTAs, liberalization through, 95–101, 100*t*
WTO service schedules, 102–103, 102*t*
Singapore–United States Free Trade
    Agreement, 41*b*
Slovenia, 124
South Africa, 2, 124, 134
Southern Common Market or
    Mercosur, 121, 124
special and differential treatment of
    developing countries, 14
stakeholders, coordination of, 27–35,
    28–30*b*, 31–33*t*, 34*f*, 35*f*, 82*n*4
Stern, Robert M., 8–9
strategic development role of trade in
    services, 1–3
    international agreements, 11–14
    liberalization, 6–11
    negotiation process, importance of
        development strategy to, 26–27
    policy making and reform,
        22–24, 24–25*b*
    special and differential treatment, 14
Sub-Saharan Africa
    diversification of exports through
        services in, 2
    European Union, agreements with, 5
    liberalization, importance of, 3
    logistics services in, 124
    openness of regime in, 8
supply capacity, enhancing, 21, 63–75
    dedicated agencies for, 73–74*b*
    identifying strengths and weaknesses of
        domestic suppliers, 67–68*b*
    key questions, 75–76*b*
    modes of supply, 74–75
    public and private sectors,
        involving, 65–72
    regulatory issues, 73, 75

service coalitions, 69–72*b*
trade-related technical assistance, 72
supply, modes of. *See* modes of supply

T

tariffs, 80
technical assistance, trade-related, 61–62,
    62–63*b*, 72
Thailand
    coordination of stakeholders
        in, 33, 34*f*, 35*f*
    diversification of exports through
        services in, 2
    health services in, 134
    logistics services in, 124
    policy-decision matrix, 33, 34*f*
Trade Facilitation Office Canada, 73–74*b*
trade in services, ix–x, 1–18
    aid for, 14, 21, 76–81. *See also* aid for
        trade in services
    database for, 5, 87–119. *See also* service
        regulations management tool
    defined, 1
    increasing tradability of, 2–3
    international agreements, strategic
        development role of, 11–14
    liberalization of. *See* liberalization of
        trade in services
    negotiation exercise, 121–170. *See also*
        negotiation exercise
    negotiations, 4–5, 19–68. *See also*
        negotiation of agreements
    policy making and reform, 4. *See also*
        policy making and reform
    regulations, 4. *See also* regulatory issues
    sequencing issues, 4–5
    strategic development role of, 1–3. *See
        also* strategic development role of
        trade in services
    training, 6. *See also* training
trade-related regulatory audits, 36–42,
    37–40*b*, 42–42*b*
trade-related technical assistance, 61–62,
    62–63*b*, 72
training, 6
    negotiation exercise. *See*
        negotiation exercise
    regulatory capacity-building,
        58–61, 59–61*b*
    trade-related technical assistance,
        61–62, 62–63*b*

Treaty of Rome (1958), 115–116n3
Tunisia, 2, 140

U

U.S. Agency for International Development
    (USAID), 60–61b
Uganda, 124
United Nations Conference on Trade and
    Development (UNCTAD), 82n2
United Nations Economic Commission for
    Latin America and the Caribbean,
    82n2
United Nations Provisional Central
    Product Classification (CPC), 131,
    163–167t
United States
    all trade agreements with now involving
        trade in services, 5, 87
    exceptions, negotiating, 12
    health services, demand for, 134–138
    Singapore–United States Free Trade
        Agreement, 41b
    USAID, 60–61b
United States International Trade
    Commission (USITC), 130
United States–Chile Free Trade
    Agreement, 111b
Uruguay, 2, 124, 129
Uruguay Round
    bilateral request-offer approach in, 47b
    broader obligations established by, 53
    logistics services, 130
    service coalitions, 69b
USITC (United States International Trade
    Commission), 130

V

Vaillant, Marcel, 87
Vietnam, 124

W

World Bank, 72, 130
World Bank Institute, 82n2
World Trade Net Program, 72b
World Trade Organization (WTO).
        See also Doha Round;
        Uruguay Round
    commitment schedules, 103–104, 104t
    conducting negotiations, 46
    countries seeking accession
        to, 83n13
    GATS. See General Agreement on Trade
        in Services
    GATT, 81, 92–94, 94t
    implementation issues, 55
    information access issues, 82–83n6
    logistic services negotiation proposal,
        131, 132–133t
    number of agreements entered into by
        members, 87
    PTAs ordered by year of notification to,
        classification of, 98, 113–115t
    service coalitions, 70b
    service schedules, 102–103, 102t
    special and differential treatment of
        developing countries, 14
    stakeholders, coordination of, 28, 30
    success of unilateral efforts versus, 20
    supply capacity, enhancing, 66
    trade-related regulatory audits, 36

ECO-AUDIT
Environmental Benefits Statement

The World Bank is committed to preserving endangered forests and natural resources. The Office of the Publisher has chosen to print *Trade in Services Negotiations* on recycled paper with 50 percent postconsumer fiber in accordance with the recommended standards for paper usage set by the Green Press Initiative, a nonprofit program supporting publishers in using fiber that is not sourced from endangered forests. For more information, visit www.greenpressinitiative.org.

Saved:
- 3 trees
- 1 million BTU's of total energy
- 323 lb. of greenhouse gases
- 1,555 gal. of waste water
- 94 lbs. of solid waste

green
press
INITIATIVE

www.ingramcontent.com/pod-product-compliance
Lightning Source LLC
Chambersburg PA
CBHW050445280326
41932CB00013BA/2249